BRITAINS LEAST USED S

DAVID BREWER

CONTENTS
2 INTRODUCTION
3-7 NOTES ON FEATURED STATIONS
8-224 INDIVIDUAL STATIONS
226 NORTHERN ENGLAND MAP
228 SOUTH EAST & EAST MIDLANDS MAP
230 WALES & SOUTH WEST MAP
232 SCOTLAND MAP
234-235 LIST OF 200 LEAST USED STATIONS
236-237 INDEX

ACKNOWLEDGEMENTS

Putting this book together has been no easy task but it has been an enjoyable and satisfying one. I am grateful to my wife Shirley for her help and encouragement, without which this book would not be possible. Thank you to my son Simon for his patience in helping me on work needed to be done on the computer and my daughter Tracey for her help in reading through the book and checking for any mistakes. I would also like to thank Dominic, Adrian and Andrew at T Snape & Co. for their efficient work in the printing and binding of this book.

This is my first attempt publishing a book and I hope you get as much pleasure in reading it as I have in compiling it.

Front Cover: Scotscalder on the Far North Line

Back Cover Top: Chathill on the East Coast Line north of Newcastle
Back Cover Bottom: Dolau on the Heart of Wales Line.

Copyright © David Brewer

Published by David Brewer Email: davidbrewer20547@aol.com

Printed and bound by T Snape & Co Ltd. Bolton's Court, Preston, Lancashire PR1 3TY.
Tel: 01772 254553.

INTRODUCTION

My interest in railways began in 1957 when my father bought me Ian Allan's ABC British Railways Locomotives Part 3 London Midland, Scottish Regions to keep me occupied on a train journey from Preston to London. Little was I to know then how this book would be the start of a lifetime interest in railways. Like many boys at that time I became a keen train spotter. My early years train spotting was spent on Preston station and trips with my parents to visit relatives in London. It was not long before I was going on trips on my own, initially to places like Crewe, Carlisle and York. As my interest in trains grew I started making trips to all parts of the country from Scotland to Cornwall and South Wales to East Anglia to visit as many engine sheds as possible. It would be a race against time to see as many steam locomotives as possible before they were withdrawn. The one regret was that I took very few photos during those trips.

Other interests included music and in 1970 I started my own retail business selling records. Working six days a week left little time for any rail trips. I got married and started a family. My rail trips were confined to Rail Open Days and Santa Specials.

I had never lost interest in railways and in 1998 I closed my business and applied for a position on the railway. After failing an interview to be a conductor with Virgin Trains I obtained a position of Ticket Office Clerk with First North Western (now Northern). The first six months were spent at Leyland station before moving to Chorley where I spent nine years before retiring in 2007. Working on the railway rekindled my interest and I started making trips to places I had visited over thirty years ago. Now I would never go anywhere without my camera. In addition to photographing trains I began to take photos of stations and set myself the task of visiting and taking photos of every station in Britain. With over 2500 stations to visit this proved no easy task and trips required careful planning. Several stations had only one or two services each day, with some only having one each week. To reach some stations with a limited service I would catch a bus from the nearest station with a regular service. On many occasions it would involve a long walk, sometimes of more than two miles.

By September 2011 I had visited and taken photos at every station on the rail network. Since then I have continued to visit stations to update my photos usually making at least one trip every week. Also once a year I use the Seven Days All Line Rover Ticket which allows unlimited travel anywhere on the rail network.

In this book we look at the least used stations in Britain. All of the 200 currently least used stations are included plus a selection of other stations with low usage numbers.

Each station is illustrated by photos which I have taken with at least one general view and one of a train calling or passing through the station. There is a brief description about each station and a chart listing facts about the station, including opening dates, service frequency and station usage.

OPENING DATES

Most of the stations featured in the book were opened in the nineteenth century. The oldest being Blaydon opened on 10 March 1835 while the newest Maesteg Ewenny Road opened on 26 October 1992. Were known the exact opening date is given but for a few stations only the month and year were recorded.

Below is a list of the ten oldest and ten newest stations featured in the book showing the line on which they are located and their opening dates.

1 Blaydon	Newcastle-Carlisle	10 March 1835
2 Norton Bridge	Stafford-Crewe	4 July 1837
3 Monifieth	Dundee- Aberdeen	8 October 1838
4 Ulleskelf	York- Leeds	30 May 1839
5 Peartree	Derby- Crewe	12 August 1839
6 Broomfleet	Hull-Sheffield	1 July 1840
7 Eastrington	Hull-York	2 July 1840
8 Wressle	Hull-York	2 July 1840
9 Salwick	Preston-Blackpool	16 July 1840
10 Ardwick	Manchester-Hadfield	November 1842

1 Maesteg Ewenny Road	Bridgend-Maesteg	26 October 1992
2 Loch Eil Outward Bound	Fort William-Mallaig	6 May 1985
3 Redcar British Steel	Middlesbrough-Saltburn	19 June 1978
4 Teesside Airport	Darlington-Middlesbrough	3 October 1971
5 Balmossie	Dundee-Aberdeen	18 June1962
6 Golf Street	Dundee-Aberdeen	7 November 1960
7 Longcross	Waterloo-Reading	21 September 1942
8 Stanlow & Thornton	Ellesmere Port-Helsby	23 December 1940
9 Wedgwood	Stoke on Trent-Stafford	1 January 1940
10 Thornford	Bristol -Weymouth	23 March 1936

Stations which have closed and been reopened include.
Dent closed between 1970-1986
Duncraig 1964-1976
Dunrobin Castle 1965-1985
Dunstan 1926-1984
Falls of Cruachan 1965-1988
Glan Conwy 1964-1970
Moss Side 1961-1983
Okehampton 1972-1997
Peartree 1968-1976
Penally 1964-1970
Rogart 1960-1961
Sampford Courtenay 1972-2002

Three stations in Scotland which when first opened were not available for public use.
Dunrobin Castle   Opened for the Castle home of the Duke of Sutherland
Duncraig   Opened to serve Duncraig Castle
Beasdale   Opened to serve Arisaig House

Britains Least Used Stations

DAYS OPENED

Most stations receive a service seven days of the week but with a reduced frequency on Sunday. Some stations are closed on Sunday. There are however exceptions.

Stations which receive a more frequent service on Sunday:
Berney Arms, Buckenham and Lakenheath in Norfolk

Stations only opened on Sunday:
Sampford Courtenay and Okehampton in Devon

Stations opened only on Saturday:
Brigg, Kirton Lindsey and Gainsborough Central on the Sheffield to Cleethorpes Line

Stations closed on Sunday during winter months:
Moss Side on the Preston to Blackpool South Line
Coombe Junction Halt, St Keyne Wishing Well Halt, Causeland and Sandplace on the Looe Valley Line
Glan Conwy, Tal-y-Cafn, Dolgarrog, North Llanwrst, Pont-y-Pant, Dolwyddelan and Roman Bridge on the Conwy Valley Line
New Clee, Grimsby Docks, Thornton Abbey and Barrow Haven on the Barton on Humber Line

Stations opened only during summer months:
Dunrobin Castle on the Far North Line
Falls of Cruachan on the Oban branch of the West Highland Line

Stations closed on summer Saturdays to allow a more frequent direct service to Newquay:
Luxulyan, Bugle, Roche, St Columb Road and Quintrel Downs on the Newquay branch

SERVICE FREQUENCY

The station with the best service is Swale on the Sittingbourne to Sheerness- on- Sea Line which has a half hourly service (hourly on Sunday).
Stations with a weekday hourly service include Ashley between Manchester and Chester, Gilfach Fargoed (Cardiff and Rhymney) Kempston Hardwick (Bedford and Bletchley) Maesteg Ewenny Road (Bridgend and Maesteg) Parton (Carlisle and Whitehaven) and South Bank (Middlesbrough and Saltburn).
While most stations receive a service every two or three hours there are some which only receive one or two trains each way on weekdays. These are mainly commuter services in the morning and afternoon peak times.
A Parliamentary Service is one which continues to run to avoid the cost of formal closure of the station and consists of only one or two trains per week.
Teesside Airport between Darlington and Middlesbrough receives one train each way on Sunday.
Pilning between Bristol Temple Meads and Cardiff Central receives one train each way on Saturday.
Denton and Reddish South between Stockport and Stalybridge receive one train per week on Friday.

Wedgwood, Barlaston and Norton Bridge between Stoke-on-Trent and Stafford have no trains calling but are served by buses.

Some stations have recently received a much improved service. These include Dunston and Blaydon on the Newcastle to Carlisle Line, South Bank on the Middlesbrough to Saltburn Line and Three Oaks and Winchelsea between Hastings and Ashford International.

LOCATION OF STATIONS

The least used stations can be found on most parts of the rail network. In England most are to be found at the following locations:

The Branch Lines of Devon and Cornwall
East Anglia around Norwich
East Midlands east of Nottingham
Humberside and Yorkshire
The North East around Middlesbrough and Newcastle
The North West

There are very few to be found around London and the South East or in the West Midlands around Birmingham.

In Wales most are to found on the following lines:
Heart of Wales Line between Shrewsbury and Swansea
Cambrian Coast Line between Machynlleth and Pwllheli
Conwy Valley Line between Llandudno and Blaenau Ffestiniog

In Scotland most are to be found on the following lines:
West Highland Line between Glasgow and Mallaig and between Glasgow and Oban
Kyle of Lochalsh Line between Inverness and Kyle
Far North Line between Inverness and Wick
Tayside around Dundee

Not all of the stations are found on Branch Lines in England or the Scenic Lines in Wales and Scotland. Stations located near to the centre of towns and cities include:
Ardwick half a mile from Manchester Piccadilly on the line to Hadfield
Peartree one and a quarter miles from Derby on the line to Crewe
Manors half a mile from Newcastle on the East Coast Main Line
Keyham two miles from Plymouth on the Gunnislake branch
Grimsby Docks one mile from Grimsby Town station

Stations located on Main Lines include:
Polesworth on the West Coast Main Line between Tamworth and Nuneaton
Norton Bridge on the West Coast Main Line four miles north of Stafford
Pegswood, Widdrington, Acklington and Chathill on the East Coast Main Line north of Newcastle
St Budeaux Ferry Road and Menheniot on the Cornish Main Line west of Plymouth

Some stations have no road access and can only be reached by foot.
Berney Arms between Norwich and Great Yarmouth. The station is over three miles from the nearest road but it can be reached by boat on the River Yare half a mile away.
Altnabraec on the Far North Line is only accessible along twenty miles of dirt track unsuitable for most vehicles.
Dovey Junction on the Cambrian Coast Line can only be reached along a three quarters of a mile long path leading from the nearest road.

Places featured in the book with more than one station.
Pontefract - In addition to Pontefract Baghill on the Sheffield to York line the town has two further stations Monkhill and Tanshelf on the Wakefield Kirkdale to Knottingly line.
Gainsborough - In addition to Gainsborough Central on the Sheffield to Cleethorpes line the town has a second station Gainsborough Lea Road on the Doncaster to Lincoln line.
Lelant - A second station Lelant Saltings half a mile away on the St Ives Bay Line opened in 1978.
St.Budeaux- In addition to St Budeaux Ferry Road on the Cornish Main Line a second station St Budeaux Victoria Road on the Gunnislake branch is situated a few yards away.
Reddish South - Reddish has a second station Reddish North half a mile away.
Tyndrum - The only place to have two stations where both are listed in the 200 least used stations in Britain. Upper Tyndrum on the West Highland Line between Glasgow and Fort William and Tyndrum Lower on the line to Oban.

Britains Least Used Stations

STATION BUILDINGS

Most stations when first opened had buildings which housed the Station Masters Office, a Ticket Office and a Waiting Room. Now with the smaller stations being unstaffed the buildings are no longer required. Some buildings have been knocked down; some remain empty while many have found further use. Most have been converted into living accommodation and are in private ownership. Many of the owners take great pride in looking after the station, furnishing them with beautiful displays of plants and flowers. Two of the best examples are Dolau on the Heart of Wales Line and Chathill north of Newcastle. Stations on the Barnstaple and Whitby Branch Lines are also well looked after.

A number of buildings have been converted into bunkhouse accommodation. These are mostly to be found in Scotland on the West Highland Line. Rogart on the Far North Line is of particular interest. The station yard has three coaches converted for this use and there is also plenty of railway memorabilia to be seen around the yard.

Some other uses of buildings are found at the following stations:
Spean Bridge on the West Highland Line has been converted into a High Class Restaurant.
Achnasheen on the Kyle of Lochalsh Line is used as a Postal Distribution Point.
Forsinard on the Far North Line is used as the visitor centre for the Royal Society for the Protection of Birds.

COMMUNITIES SERVED

The communities served by the least used stations vary in size from towns with a population of over twenty thousand to tiny hamlets with only one or two houses.
Stations serving the largest towns:
Pontefract Baghill on a line between Sheffield and York
Gainsborough Central and Brigg on a line between Sheffield and Cleethorpes
Monifieth six and a half miles north east of Dundee on the line to Aberdeen
Blaydon five and a half miles west of Newcastle on the line to Carlisle

Stations serving the smallest communities or with no settlement nearby are mostly to be found on the Scenic Lines in Wales and Scotland.
Some examples in Wales:
Roman Bridge and Dolgarrog on the Conwy Valley Line
Cynghordy and Llangynllo on the Heart of Wales Line
Tonfanau and Tygwyn on the Cambrian Coast Line

Some examples in Scotland:
Locheilside and Beasdale on the West Highland Line
Achanalt and Duncraig on the Kyle of Lochalsh Line
Kildonan and Altnabraec on the Far North Line

Some examples in England:
Coombe Junction Halt on the Looe Valley Line
Swale on the Sheerness-on-Sea branch
Shippea Hill seven miles east of Ely
Havenhouse three miles south west of Skegness
Braystones on the Cambrian Coast Line

Stations which are used principally by workers:
Salwick between Preston and Blackpool used for workers at the British Nuclear Fuel Complex
Stanlow & Thornton between Helsby and Ellesmere Port for workers at the Stanlow Refinery
Redcar British Steel between Middlesbrough and Saltburn for workers at the Teeside Steelworks

Stations which serve passengers for other uses:
Penychain on the Cambrian Coast Line serves the Haven Holiday Park formally Butlins Holiday Camp
Loch Eil Outward Bound on the West Highland Line serves the Outward Bound Centre

There is a chart with facts about each station as explained below.

OPENED
Most stations were opened in the mid nineteenth century and the date, month and year are shown. For a few stations only the month and year are known.

PRE-GROUPING
The Railway Company the station belonged to on 1st January 1923 before the grouping to the Big 4 (LNER, LMS, GWR and S.R.) took place.

MANAGED BY
The Train Operating Company currently managing the station.

PLATFORMS
Number of platforms. Stations with staggered or island platforms are shown.

REQUEST STOP
Around half of the stations featured in the book are request stops. At these stations passengers wishing to join the train should give a clear hand signal at the station. Those wishing to alight should inform the guard.

SERVICE FREQUENCY
The number of trains that currently call at the station. These figures have been split into Weekdays, Saturdays and Sundays as follows:-

- A   A service every hour or less
- B   A service every two to three hours
- C   Between two and five services a day
- D   One service a day
- E   One service a week
- X   No service

STATION USAGE
The number of passengers using the station (entries & exits) the figures are issued by the Office of Rail Regulation and cover a period of six years.

The least used column gives the position of usage of each station. e.g. (Buckenham with 80 passengers was the seventh least used station in 2013/4).

The stations are covered in the order they appear in the rail timetable, starting north east of London and radiating anti-clockwise around England and Wales, followed by Scottish stations from south to north.

MAPS
The location of each featured station can be found on one of the four maps:
1 Northern England
2 South East and East Midlands
3 Wales and South West
4 Scotland
The number after each station in the index refers to the map on which that station can be found.

Britains Least Used Stations

BUCKENHAM

OPENED	1 MAY 1844
PRE GROUPING	GREAT EASTERN
MANAGED BY	GREATER ANGLIA
PLATFORMS	2 (STAGGERED)
REQUEST STOP	YES
SERVICE	MON-FRI SAT SUN
FREQUENCY	X E C
STATION	NUMBER OF LEAST
USAGE	PASSENGERS USED
2008/09	132 10
2009/10	154 7
2010/11	106 12
2011/12	100 9
2012/13	72 =6
2013/14	80 7

Buckenham station is situated on the Norwich to Lowestoft line eight miles from Norwich. It serves the small village of Buckenham which lies to the north of the station. There are no trains scheduled to call on weekdays with one each way on Saturday and four each way on Sunday. With around one hundred passengers using the station each year Buckenham is one of the least used stations on the rail network.

The platforms are over one hundred yards apart. The Lowestoft bound platform is just visible in the background. (right)

Greater Anglia provide the services using Classes 153, 156 or 170. 153309 departs with the 13.36 Norwich-Great Yarmouth via Berney Arms on Sunday 31 July 2011. (below)

On the same date 156422 hurries through the station with the 15.50 Lowestoft- Norwich. (below right)

Britains Least Used Stations

BERNEY ARMS

OPENED	1 MAY 1844
PRE GROUPING	GREAT EASTERN
MANAGED BY	GREATER ANGLIA
PLATFORMS	1
REQUEST STOP	YES
SERVICE	MON-FRI SAT SUN
FREQUENCY	C C B

STATION USAGE	NUMBER OF PASSENGERS	LEAST USED
2008/09	1038	66
2009/10	1628	89
2010/11	1686	88
2011/12	1436	78
2012/13	1054	=59
2013/14	1510	74

Berney Arms station is situated on the line between Norwich and Great Yarmouth via Reedham. It is one of the remotest stations in England the nearest road access being over three miles away. The Berney Arms Public House is one mile from the station. Currently two trains in each direction call Monday to Saturday with five each way on Sunday.

On 31 July 2011 Greater Anglia Class 153 153309 is seen departing with the 13.36 Norwich-Great Yarmouth. (below)

Around one hour later the same unit arrives with the 14.20 from Great Yarmouth to pick up passengers on its return working to Norwich. (below right)

Britains Least Used Stations

SPOONER ROW

OPENED	30 JULY 1845
PRE GROUPING	GREAT EASTERN
MANAGED BY	GREATER ANGLIA
PLATFORMS	2 (STAGGERED)
REQUEST STOP	YES
SERVICE	MON-FRI SAT SUN
FREQUENCY	C D X

STATION USAGE	NUMBER OF PASSENGERS	LEAST USED
2008/09	718	51
2009/10	616	46
2010/11	640	45
2011/12	338	27
2012/13	264	23
2013/14	388	30

Spooner Row station is situated on the Norwich to Ely line between Wymondham and Attleborough. The station serves the village of Spooner Row.

The level crossing used to be operated manually by the signalman from the signal box. In 2012 the signal box was closed and the crossing replaced by automated full barriers with flashing warning lights.(right)

On Weekday's there are two trains to Norwich in the morning and one in the afternoon to Cambridge. Greater Anglia Class 170s are provided on these services. 170272 is seen departing with the 9.12 Cambridge-Norwich on 16 July 2014.(below)

East Midland services to Norwich pass through the station. 158774 approaches the level crossing with the 7.52 Nottingham-Norwich on 16 July 2014. (below right)

10   Britains Least Used Stations

ECCLES ROAD

OPENED	30 JULY 1845
PRE GROUPING	GREAT EASTERN
MANAGED BY	GREATER ANGLIA
PLATFORMS	2
REQUEST STOP	NO
SERVICE	MON-FRI SAT SUN
FREQUENCY	C C X

STATION USAGE	NUMBER OF PASSENGERS	LEAST USED
2008/09	1966	112
2009/10	1796	98
2010/11	1676	87
2011/12	1242	62
2012/13	1930	93
2013/14	2126	100

Eccles Road station is situated on the Norwich to Ely line 19 miles west of Norwich. A village called Eccles used to be located one mile south of the station hence the name Eccles Road.

Eccles Road receives two morning trains to Norwich and two afternoon trains from Norwich. 170207 passes with the 14.40 Norwich-Cambridge on 30 July 2011.

On the same date 158847 hurries through Eccles Road with the 14.57 Norwich-Liverpool Lime Street.

Britains Least Used Stations

HARLING ROAD

OPENED	30 JULY 1845
PRE GROUPING	GREAT EASTERN
MANAGED BY	GREATER ANGLIA
PLATFORMS	2
REQUEST STOP	NO
SERVICE	MON-FRI SAT SUN
FREQUENCY	C C X

STATION USAGE	NUMBER OF PASSENGERS	LEAST USED
2008/09	4152	172
2009/10	3900	162
2010/11	3494	148
2011/12	4224	159
2012/13	3592	146
2013/14	3222	132

Harling Road station is situated on the Norwich to Ely line eight miles east of Thetford and 23 miles west of Norwich. The station was opened as Harling and renamed Harling Road four years later. The village of East Harling is located two miles from the station.

Harling Road receives the same service as Eccles Road. On 30 July 2011 170204 calls with the 15.35 Norwich-Cambridge.

On the same date 158863 is seen speeding through Harling Road with the 15.52 Norwich - Liverpool Lime Street.

Britains Least Used Stations

LAKENHEATH

OPENED	30 JULY 1845
PRE GROUPING	GREAT EASTERN
MANAGED BY	GREATER ANGLIA
PLATFORMS	2
REQUEST STOP	YES
SERVICE	MON-FRI SAT SUN
FREQUENCY	X D C

STATION USAGE	NUMBER OF PASSENGERS	LEAST USED
2008/09	536	39
2009/10	370	30
2010/11	404	33
2011/12	390	34
2012/13	440	31
2013/14	378	29

Lakenheath station is situated twelve miles east of Ely on the line to Norwich. The village of Lakenheath lies three miles to the south of the station. There is no sizeable population within walking distance and the station is mainly used for visiting the nearby Royal Society for the Protection of Birds Nature Reserve at Lakenheath Fen.

A view looking in the direction of Norwich showing the manual crossing gates and signal box.

Lakenheath receives no weekday service, one train each way on Saturday and three each way on Sunday. On Sunday 31 July 2011 170207 pulls into the station with the 10.48 Cambridge-Norwich.

Britains Least Used Stations

SHIPPEA HILL

OPENED	30 JULY 1845
PRE GROUPING	GREAT EASTERN
MANAGED BY	GREATER ANGLIA
PLATFORMS	2
REQUEST STOP	YES
SERVICE	MON-FRI SAT SUN
FREQUENCY	D D X

STATION USAGE	NUMBER OF PASSENGERS	LEAST USED
2008/09	868	57
2009/10	942	58
2010/11	812	=52
2011/12	376	=29
2012/13	50	3
2013/14	12	2

Shippea Hill station opened as Mildenhall Road was renamed Burnt Fen in 1885 and finally Shippea Hill in 1905. It is situated seven miles east of Ely on the A1101 road between Littleport and Mildenhall. There is no settlement within walking distance. Only 12 passengers used the station in 2013/14 making it currently the second least used station on the rail network.

Shippea Hill receives one train weekdays and one each way on Saturday. 170204 arrives with the 18.40 Norwich-Cambridge on 30 July 2011.

14   Britains Least Used Stations

MANEA

OPENED	14 JANUARY 1847
PRE GROUPING	GREAT EASTERN
MANAGED BY	GREATER ANGLIA
PLATFORMS	2
REQUEST STOP	YES
SERVICE FREQUENCY	MON-FRI SAT SUN B B X

STATION USAGE	NUMBER OF PASSENGERS	LEAST USED
2008/09	3048	144
2009/10	2596	130
2010/11	3368	145
2011/12	3050	134
2012/13	2898	130
2013/14	3694	138

Manea station is on the Norwich to Peterborough line between Ely and March. It serves the village of Manea located to the south of the station. The station had a reprieve in 1966 when British Rail's request it should be closed was turned down by the then Minister for Transport Barbara Castle.

Until the end of 2013 Manea only received two trains in each direction on Cross Country Services. Now in addition, Greater Anglia services between Ipswich and Peterborough provide a two hourly service.
170115 calls with the 17.18 Stanstead Airport-Birmingham New Street on 2 September 2011.

On the same date 158780 passes at speed with the 15.52 Norwich-Liverpool Lime Street.

Britains Least Used Stations

HAVENHOUSE

OPENED	28 JULY 1873
PRE GROUPING	GREAT NORTHERN
MANAGED BY	EAST MIDLANDS
PLATFORMS	2
REQUEST STOP	NO
SERVICE	MON-FRI SAT SUN
FREQUENCY	C C X

STATION USAGE	NUMBER OF PASSENGERS	LEAST USED
2008/09	328	29
2009/10	378	31
2010/11	100	11
2011/12	132	11
2012/13	226	19
2013/14	278	21

Havenhouse station is situated three miles south west of Skegness on the line to Nottingham. There is no immediate settlement nearby.

The station opened as Croft Bank and was renamed Havenhouse in 1900.

East Midland Class 158 No 158865 nears the end of its journey with the 10.45 Nottingham-Skegness on 10 June 2011.

Britains Least Used Stations

THORPE CULVERT

OPENED	24 OCTOBER 1871
PRE GROUPING	GREAT NORTHERN
MANAGED BY	EAST MIDLANDS
PLATFORMS	2
REQUEST STOP	NO
SERVICE	MON-FRI SAT SUN
FREQUENCY	C C X

STATION USAGE	NUMBER OF PASSENGERS	LEAST USED
2008/09	960	60
2009/10	382	33
2010/11	418	34
2011/12	340	28
2012/13	352	28
2013/14	340	26

Thorpe Culvert station is on the Nottingham to Skegness line 17 miles north east of Boston. The nearest village is Thorpe St Peter situated half a mile from the station.

Only two trains call in each direction. 156411 arrives with the 16.11 Skegness- Nottingham on 10 June 2011.

On the same date 158783/153326 are seen passing with 12.45 Nottingham-Skegness.

Britains Least Used Stations 17

HUBBERTS BRIDGE

OPENED	JUNE 1860
PRE GROUPING	GREAT NORTHERN
MANAGED BY	EAST MIDLANDS
PLATFORMS	2
REQUEST STOP	NO
SERVICE FREQUENCY	MON-FRI SAT SUN C C X

STATION USAGE	NUMBER OF PASSENGERS	LEAST USED
2008/09	558	42
2009/10	296	=25
2010/11	342	=28
2011/12	692	=43
2012/13	590	38
2013/14	334	25

Hubberts Bridge station is on the Nottingham to Skegness line four miles west of Boston. It serves the small village of Hubberts Bridge.

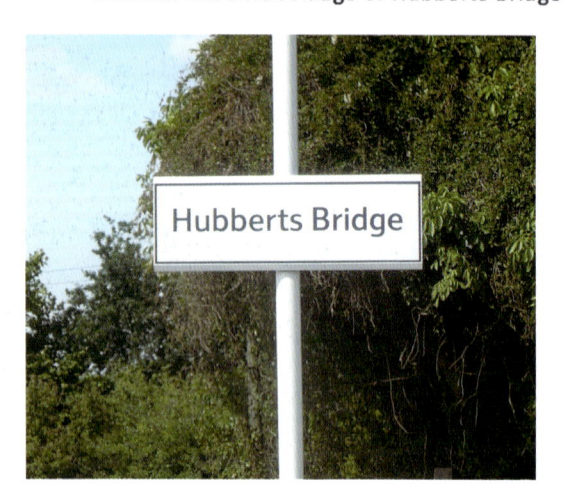

The distinctive signal box and level crossing are seen at the west of the station.

Hubberts Bridge only receives two trains in each direction. Two East Midland Class 158s headed by 158863 are seen speeding through the station with the 14.15 Skegness-Nottingham on 14 June 2011.

18   *Britains Least Used Stations*

SWINESHEAD

OPENED	13 APRIL 1859
PRE GROUPING	GREAT NORTHERN
MANAGED BY	EAST MIDLANDS
PLATFORMS	2
REQUEST STOP	NO
SERVICE	MON-FRI SAT SUN
FREQUENCY	C C X

STATION USAGE	NUMBER OF PASSENGERS	LEAST USED
2008/09	1028	=65
2009/10	1312	72
2010/11	2378	120
2011/12	2260	110
2012/13	3192	135
2013/14	3294	134

Swineshead station is on the Nottingham to Skegness line between Sleaford and Boston. The station is located in the hamlet of Swineshead Bridge and two miles north of the village of Swineshead.

The station building appears to be in private ownership.

158785 calls at Swineshead with the 15.09 Skegness-Nottingham on 14 June 2011.

Britains Least Used Stations

RAUCEBY

OPENED	1 OCTOBER 1881
PRE GROUPING	GREAT NORTHERN
MANAGED BY	GREATER ANGLIA
PLATFORMS	2
REQUEST STOP	NO
SERVICE	MON-FRI SAT SUN
FREQUENCY	C C X

STATION USAGE	NUMBER OF PASSENGERS	LEAST USED
2008/09	1788	103
2009/10	1970	=106
2010/11	1822	92
2011/12	1828	92
2012/13	2350	114
2013/14	1898	90

Rauceby station is on the Nottingham to Skegness line three miles west of Sleaford. It is situated half a mile south of the village of South Rauceby. It is believed that Nick Clegg proposed to his wife on the platform while waiting for a train to Sleaford.

The signal box and manually operated crossing gates can be seen at the western end of the platform.

Monday to Saturday sees three trains call in each direction provided by East Midlands Trains. On 14 June 2011 153374/158875 pass with the 10.45 Nottingham-Skegness.

Britains Least Used Stations

ELTON & ORSTON

OPENED	15 JULY 1850
PRE GROUPING	GREAT NORTHERN
MANAGED BY	EAST MIDLANDS
PLATFORMS	2
REQUEST STOP	NO
SERVICE	MON-FRI SAT SUN
FREQUENCY	D D X

STATION USAGE	NUMBER OF PASSENGERS	LEAST USED
2008/09	172	12
2009/10	166	=10
2010/11	84	=9
2011/12	72	6
2012/13	72	=6
2013/14	166	15

Elton & Orston station is 14 miles east of Nottingham on the line to Skegness. It opened as Elton and became Elton & Orston in 1904. The station is situated midway between the two villages around one mile from each.

With around one hundred passengers using the station each year Elton & Orston is one of the least used stations. An East Midlands Class 158 passes with the 14.45 Nottingham-Skegness on 15 October 2009.

Only one early morning service to Nottingham and one late afternoon service to Skegness call at Elton & Orston. On 15 October 2009 158788 hurries through the station with the 11.52 Liverpool Lime Street-Norwich.

Britains Least Used Stations 21

NETHERFIELD

OPENED	MAY 1878
PRE GROUPING	GREAT NORTHERN
MANAGED BY	EAST MIDLANDS
PLATFORMS	2 (ISLAND)
REQUEST STOP	NO
SERVICE	MON-FRI SAT SUN
FREQUENCY	C C C

STATION USAGE	NUMBER OF PASSENGERS	LEAST USED
2008/09	8292	=247
2009/10	6412	214
2010/11	6132	201
2011/12	7410	212
2012/13	6628	202
2013/14	5382	181

Netherfield station is on the Nottingham to Skegness Line three miles east of Nottingham. The station opened as Colwick became Netherfield and Colwick in 1925 and Netherfield in 1974. Carlton station on the Lincoln Line is only quarter of a mile away and has a regular service to Nottingham while Netherfield only receives a peak hour service.

East Midland Class 158 no 158857 heads towards Nottingham with the 12.57 Norwich-Liverpool Lime Street on 18 February 2015.

On the same date 153308/302 arrive with the 15.45 Nottingham-Skegness.

22   Britains Least Used Stations

ROLLESTON

OPENED	1 JULY 1847
PRE GROUPING	MIDLAND
MANAGED BY	EAST MIDLANDS
PLATFORMS	2
REQUEST STOP	NO
SERVICE	MON-FRI SAT SUN
FREQUENCY	B B C

STATION USAGE	NUMBER OF PASSENGERS	LEAST USED
2008/09	7434	232
2009/10	5734	201
2010/11	4244	169
2011/12	4294	161
2012/13	3586	145
2013/14	4162	155

Rolleston station is on the Nottingham to Lincoln line three and a half miles west of Newark Castle station. It was known as Rolleston Junction until 1973 as it used to be the junction of a line to Mansfield which closed in 1959. The station is located half a mile from the village of Rolleston and adjacent to Southwell Racecourse.

The entrance to Southwell Racecourse is to the right of the picture through the level crossing.

East Midland Class 156 provide most of the services on the line. 156498 is seen passing with the 11.26 Leicester-Lincoln on 12 March 2014.

Britains Least Used Stations 23

BLEASBY

OPENED	1 OCTOBER 1850
PRE GROUPING	MIDLAND
MANAGED BY	EAST MIDLANDS
PLATFORMS	2 (STAGGERED)
REQUEST STOP	NO
SERVICE FREQUENCY	MON-FRI SAT SUN B B C

STATION USAGE	NUMBER OF PASSENGERS	LEAST USED
2008/09	5140	192
2009/10	4614	180
2010/11	3852	157
2011/12	4058	153
2012/13	4920	172
2013/14	3798	141

Bleasby station is on the Nottingham to Lincoln line eleven miles north east of Nottingham. The station serves the village of Bleasby located to the south of the station.

The station has staggered platforms some distance apart. The Lincoln bound platform is just visible in the background.

East Midlands Trains provide a two hourly service. 156408 approaches Bleasby with 12.26 Leicester-Lincoln on 12 March 2014.

THURGARTON

OPENED	4 AUGUST 1846
PRE GROUPING	MIDLAND
MANAGED BY	EAST MIDLANDS
PLATFORMS	2 (STAGGERED)
REQUEST STOP	NO
SERVICE	MON-FRI SAT SUN
FREQUENCY	B B C

STATION USAGE	NUMBER OF PASSENGERS	LEAST USED
2008/09	2938	141
2009/10	2102	=115
2010/11	2242	112
2011/12	1840	95
2012/13	2314	111
2013/14	1972	95

Thurgarton station is on the Nottingham to Lincoln line ten miles north east of Nottingham. The village of Thurgarton is situated to the north of the station. The station had parallel platforms until 1982. When the crossing was converted to automatic half barriers a new platform was built on the opposite side of the crossing.

Thurgarton receives the same service as Bleasby. 156410 is seen departing with the 12.25 Leicester-Lincoln on 12 May 2009.

On 12 March 2014 156408 enters the station with the 16.26 Leicester-Lincoln. .

Britains Least Used Stations

BURTON JOYCE

OPENED	4 AUGUST 1846
PRE GROUPING	MIDLAND
MANAGED BY	EAST MIDLANDS
PLATFORMS	2
REQUEST STOP	NO
SERVICE	MON-FRI SAT SUN
FREQUENCY	B B C
STATION	NUMBER OF LEAST
USAGE	PASSENGERS USED
2008/09	7782	239
2009/10	5760	202
2010/11	7400	224
2011/12	6786	202
2012/13	6928	204
2013/14	5302	180

Burton Joyce station is on the Nottingham to Lincoln line five miles north east of Nottingham. The village of Burton Joyce which lies on the River Trent is situated to the north of the station.

156408 calls with the 14.33 Lincoln-Leicester on 12 March 2014.

One hour later 158864 is seen passing with the 15.30 Lincoln-Leicester.

Britains Least Used Stations

NEW CLEE

OPENED	1 JULY 1875
PRE GROUPING	GREAT CENTRAL
MANAGED BY	NORTHERN
PLATFORMS	1
REQUEST STOP	YES
SERVICE	MON-FRI SAT SUN
FREQUENCY	C C C
	(X SUNDAY WINTER)

STATION USAGE	NUMBER OF PASSENGERS	LEAST USED
2008/09	526	=37
2009/10	322	27
2010/11	298	26
2011/12	334	26
2012/13	290	25
2013/14	348	27

New Clee station is situated between Grimsby Town and Cleethorpes. Originally the station had two platforms. In 1993 the line was singled and one platform removed.

New Clee is served by Northern Rail with services to Barton-on-Humber. 153317 is ready to leave with the 9.57 Barton-on-Humber-Cleethorpes on 8 October 2013.

On the same date 170305 nears the end of its journey as it passes with the 7.53 Manchester Airport-Cleethorpes.

Britains Least Used Stations

GRIMSBY DOCKS

OPENED	6 APRIL 1863
PRE GROUPING	GREAT CENTRAL
MANAGED BY	NORTHERN
PLATFORMS	1
REQUEST STOP	NO
SERVICE	MON-FRI SAT SUN
FREQUENCY	B B C
	(X SUNDAY WINTER)
STATION	NUMBER OF LEAST
USAGE	PASSENGERS USED
2008/09	5568 199
2009/10	3792 157
2010/11	3998 =163
2011/12	4068 154
2012/13	3994 156
2013/14	4662 164

Grimsby Docks station is situated one mile east of Grimsby Town station. It serves the towns commercial and fish docks area.

Grimsby Docks is served by Northern Rail on services to Barton-on-Humber. 153317 pauses with the 9.57 Barton-on-Humber-Cleethorpes on 8 October 2013.

With the Docks office building in the background First TransPennine 185116 is seen passing with the 10.26 Cleethorpes-Manchester Airport on 8 October 2013.

Britains Least Used Stations

THORNTON ABBEY

OPENED	AUGUST 1849
PRE GROUPING	GREAT CENTRAL
MANAGED BY	NORTHERN
PLATFORMS	2
REQUEST STOP	NO
SERVICE	MON-FRI SAT SUN
FREQUENCY	B B C
	(X SUNDAY WINTER)
STATION USAGE	NUMBER OF PASSENGERS LEAST USED
2008/09	1102 69
2009/10	1056 62
2010/11	1194 67
2011/12	1350 70
2012/13	954 53
2013/14	1298 61

Thornton Abbey station is on the line between Cleethorpes and Barton-on-Humber. The station is situated near to Thornton Abbey and about one mile from the village of Thornton Curtis.

On 8 October 2013 153317 calls with the 11.52 Barton-on-Humber-Cleethorpes.

Northern Rail provide Class 153 DMUs for services on the line. 153317 is seen arriving with the 12.55 Cleethorpes-Barton-on-Humber on 8 October 2013.

Britains Least Used Stations

BARROW HAVEN

OPENED	8 APRIL 1850
PRE GROUPING	GREAT CENTRAL
MANAGED BY	NORTHERN
PLATFORMS	1
REQUEST STOP	NO
SERVICE	MON-FRI SAT SUN
FREQUENCY	B B C
	(X SUNDAY WINTER)
STATION	NUMBER OF LEAST
USAGE	PASSENGERS USED
2008/09	2734 135
2009/10	2168 118
2010/11	1906 =97
2011/12	1776 89
2012/13	1744 86
2013/14	2128 101

Barrow Haven is the final intermediate station on the line between Cleethorpes and Barton-on-Humber. The station serves the villages of Barrow Haven and Barrow-upon-Humber.

The line has a two hourly service on weekdays. Sunday sees four trains each way in the summer but none in winter. 153317 calls with the 10.55 Cleethorpes-Barton-on-Humber on 8 October 2013.

After a nine minute turnaround at Barton-on-Humber the same unit returns with the 11.52 to Cleethorpes.

Britains Least Used Stations

BROOMFLEET

OPENED	1 JULY 1840
PRE GROUPING	NORTH EASTERN
MANAGED BY	NORTHERN
PLATFORMS	2
REQUEST STOP	NO
SERVICE	MON-FRI SAT SUN
FREQUENCY	C C X

STATION USAGE	NUMBER OF PASSENGERS	LEAST USED
2008/09	2494	129
2009/10	2572	128
2010/11	2106	108
2011/12	1562	83
2012/13	1608	78
2013/14	1326	64

Broomfleet station is on the Hull to Sheffield line 15 miles west of Hull. The station serves the village of Bloomfleet which has a population of around 300.

Broomfleet has a limited service of four trains in each direction provided by Northern. On 1 April 2014 158790 calls with the 14.54 Scarborough-Doncaster.

TransPennine services between Hull and Manchester pass the station. 185125 speeds through with the 16.40 Hull-Manchester Piccadilly on 23 April 2013.

Britains Least Used Stations 31

EASTRINGTON

OPENED	2 JULY 1840
PRE GROUPING	NORTH EASTERN
MANAGED BY	NORTHERN
PLATFORMS	2
REQUEST STOP	NO
SERVICE	MON-FRI SAT SUN
FREQUENCY	C C X

STATION USAGE	NUMBER OF PASSENGERS	LEAST USED
2008/09	672	49
2009/10	1380	75
2010/11	1886	95
2011/12	1204	61
2012/13	1446	69
2013/14	1738	84

Eastrington station is on the Hull to York line 20 miles west of Hull. The station was known as South Eastrington between 1922 and 1961 to distinguish it from North Eastrington a station on a line between Hull and Barnsley which closed in 1955.

Eastrington receives three trains in each direction on weekdays. 158901 calls with the 17.18 Hull-York on 1 April 2014.

On the same date 170306 speeds through Eastrington with the 17.58 Hull - Manchester Piccadilly.

Britains Least Used Stations

WRESSLE

OPENED	2 JULY 1840
PRE GROUPING	NORTH EASTERN
MANAGED BY	NORTHERN
PLATFORMS	2
REQUEST STOP	NO
SERVICE	MON-FRI SAT SUN
FREQUENCY	C C X
STATION	NUMBER OF LEAST
USAGE	PASSENGERS USED
2008/09	1384 88
2009/10	1834 101
2010/11	1594 81
2011/12	1306 68
2012/13	1488 71
2013/14	1548 =75

Wressle station is on the Hull to York line 25 miles from Hull and six miles east of Selby. The village of Wressle has a population of under 300 and lies to the north of the station.

Northern Class 158 provide most of the services. On 23 April 2013 158784/843 approach Wressle with the 18.18 York-Hull.

170306/301 are seen passing with the 16.42 Manchester Piccadilly-Hull TransPennine service on 23 April 2013.

Britains Least Used Stations

33

SALTMARSHE

OPENED	2 AUGUST 1869
PRE GROUPING	NORTH EASTERN
MANAGED BY	NORTHERN
PLATFORMS	2
REQUEST STOP	NO
SERVICE FREQUENCY	MON-FRI SAT SUN B B X

STATION USAGE	NUMBER OF PASSENGERS	LEAST USED
2008/09	4150	171
2009/10	4196	171
2010/11	3664	152
2011/12	4470	164
2012/13	4280	160
2013/14	3524	136

Saltmarshe station is on the Hull to Sheffield line three miles north east of Goole. It serves the villages of Laxton and Saltmarshe.

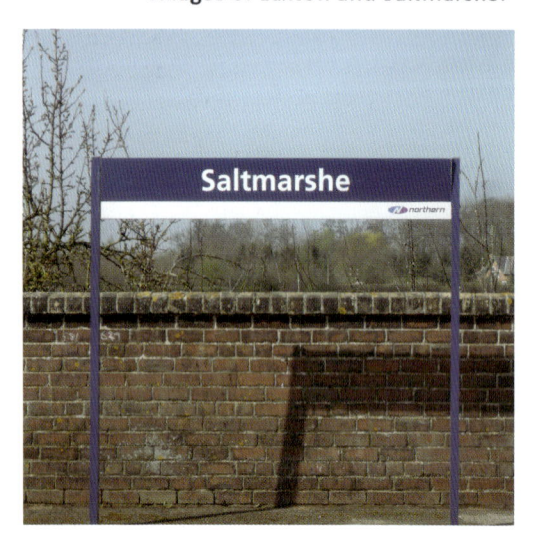

Saltmarshe has a weekly service of six trains in each direction mainly during the morning and afternoon peaks. 158795 is seen approaching the station with the 16.46 Doncaster-Bridlington on 31 March 2009.

On 1 April 2014 158817 speeds through the station with the 13.11 Bridlington-Sheffield.

34 Britains Least Used Stations

ALTHORPE

OPENED	1 OCTOBER 1866
PRE GROUPING	NORTH EASTERN
MANAGED BY	NORTHERN
PLATFORMS	2
REQUEST STOP	NO
SERVICE	MON-FRI SAT SUN
FREQUENCY	A A X

STATION USAGE	NUMBER OF PASSENGERS	LEAST USED
2008/09	8906	256
2009/10	6700	220
2010/11	8430	234
2011/12	9296	240
2012/13	8476	230
2013/14	6404	193

Althorpe station is on the line between Doncaster and Grimsby three and a half miles west of Scunthorpe. The station is situated between the villages of Althorpe, Keadby and Gunness on the west bank of the River Trent. The station which was originally known as Keadby and Althorpe was resited in May 1916. A landslip at Hatfield Colliery in February 2013 caused the line to be closed for five months hence the reduced number of passengers using the station.

The King George V Bridge over the River Trent can be seen in the background as 142086 approaches Althorpe with the 13.19 Scunthorpe-Lincoln (via Sheffield) on 29 April 2014.

TransPennine services to Cleethorpes pass through the station. 185139 is seen with the 10.55 Manchester Airport-Cleethorpes on 29 April 2014.

Britains Least Used Stations

GAINSBOROUGH CENTRAL

OPENED	2 APRIL 1849
PRE GROUPING	GREAT CENTRAL
MANAGED BY	NORTHERN
PLATFORMS	2
REQUEST STOP	NO
SERVICE	MON-FRI SAT SUN
FREQUENCY	X C X

STATION USAGE	NUMBER OF PASSENGERS	LEAST USED
2008/09	1172	77
2009/10	1438	77
2010/11	1134	65
2011/12	1348	69
2012/13	1128	63
2013/14	1220	=58

Gainsborough Central station is on the Sheffield to Cleethorpes line ten miles north east of Retford. There is a busier station at Gainsborough Lea Road which is on the Doncaster to Lincoln line.

There are no weekday or Sunday services with just three trains in each direction on Saturday. 153358 pauses at the station with the 11.13 Cleethorpes-Sheffield on 19 June 2010.

On the same date 153315 arrives with the 12.00 Sheffield-Cleethorpes.

36 Britains Least Used Stations

KIRTON LINDSEY

OPENED	2 APRIL 1849
PRE GROUPING	GREAT CENTRAL
MANAGED BY	NORTHERN
PLATFORMS	1
REQUEST STOP	NO
SERVICE	MON-FRI SAT SUN
FREQUENCY	X C X

STATION USAGE	NUMBER OF PASSENGERS	LEAST USED
2008/09	88	4
2009/10	220	17
2010/11	224	22
2011/12	210	18
2012/13	186	17
2013/14	120	11

Kirton Lindsey station is on the Sheffield to Cleethorpes line between Gainsborough Central and Brigg. It serves the small town of Kirton in Lindsey which is situated half a mile from the station.

The station building appears to be in private ownership.

Northern Rail Class 153 are used for services on the line. 153315 calls with the 12.00 Sheffield-Cleethorpes on 19 June 2010.

Britains Least Used Stations 37

BRIGG

OPENED	1 NOVEMBER 1848
PRE GROUPING	GREAT CENTRAL
MANAGED BY	NORTHERN
PLATFORMS	2
REQUEST STOP	NO
SERVICE	MON-FRI SAT SUN
FREQUENCY	X C X

STATION USAGE	NUMBER OF PASSENGERS	LEAST USED
2008/09	554	41
2009/10	414	37
2010/11	702	48
2011/12	692	=43
2012/13	794	48
2013/14	922	50

Brigg station is situated on the Sheffield to Cleethorpes line. The station serves the town of Brigg which has a population of over 5000. Along with Gainsborough Central and Kirton Lindsey it has a Saturday only service of three trains in each direction. A regular weekday service would increase the low usage figures of Brigg as well as at Gainsborough Central and Kirton Lindsey.

153315 calls at Brigg on 19 June 2010 with the 12.00 Sheffield-Cleethorpes.

Britains Least Used Stations

WHITLEY BRIDGE

OPENED	1 APRIL 1848
PRE GROUPING	LANCASHIRE & YORKSHIRE
MANAGED BY	NORTHERN
PLATFORMS	2
REQUEST STOP	NO
SERVICE FREQUENCY	MON-FRI SAT SUN C C X

STATION USAGE	NUMBER OF PASSENGERS	LEAST USED
2008/09	950	59
2009/10	680	=51
2010/11	904	54
2011/12	980	56
2012/13	1270	66
2013/14	864	47

Whitley Bridge station is situated on the Leeds to Goole line four miles east of Knottingley. It serves the villages of Eggborough to the north of the station and Whitley to the south.

The station receives a limited service of one morning and one evening train to Leeds and one morning train to Goole. Services are provided by Northern Rail which normally consists of a Class 150 coupled to a Class 153. 150215/153316 arrive at Whitley Bridge with the 17.16 Leeds-Goole on 29 April 2014.

The line sees plenty of freight traffic. On 29 April 2014 four Class 66 hauled freights were seen passing in a period of one hour. One of these 66084 heads towards the nearby Drax Power Station.

Britains Least Used Stations

HENSALL

OPENED	1 APRIL 1848
PRE GROUPING	LANCASHIRE & YORKSHIRE
MANAGED BY	NORTHERN
PLATFORMS	2
REQUEST STOP	NO
SERVICE	MON-FRI SAT SUN
FREQUENCY	C C X

STATION USAGE	NUMBER OF PASSENGERS	LEAST USED
2008/09	266	26
2009/10	326	29
2010/11	254	25
2011/12	184	15
2012/13	272	24
2013/14	276	20

Hensall station is situated on the line between Leeds and Goole six miles east of Knottingley. The village of Hensall lies to the north of the station.

The station building is in private ownership and has many old fashioned advertisements on its walls.

The trolleys on the platform and the old sign are a reminder of the stations L & Y origins.

40

Britains Least Used Stations

HENSALL

The station has one of the last set of electrical wheel gates in the country. (right)

153316/150215 run into Hensall on 29 April 2014 with 18.49 Goole-Leeds. (middle)

153363/150274 are ready to depart with the 17.16 Leeds-Goole on 30 April 2010. (bottom)

Britains Least Used Stations

SNAITH

OPENED	1 APRIL 1848
PRE GROUPING	LANCASHIRE & YORKSHIRE
MANAGED BY	NORTHERN
PLATFORMS	1
REQUEST STOP	NO
SERVICE FREQUENCY	MON-FRI SAT SUN C C X

STATION USAGE	NUMBER OF PASSENGERS	LEAST USED
2008/09	2870	139
2009/10	2574	129
2010/11	2994	138
2011/12	1738	88
2012/13	1808	90
2013/14	1776	85

Snaith station is on the Leeds-Goole line ten miles east of Knottingley and seven miles west of Goole. It serves the small town of Snaith which has a population of around 3000.

On 30 April 2010 153363 coupled to 150270 depart with the 17.16 Leeds- Goole.

Later that day the same units are seen returning with the 18.49 Goole-Leeds.

Britains Least Used Stations

RAWCLIFFE

OPENED	1 APRIL 1848
PRE GROUPING	LANCASHIRE & YORKSHIRE
MANAGED BY	NORTHERN
PLATFORMS	1
REQUEST STOP	NO
SERVICE	MON-FRI SAT SUN
FREQUENCY	C C X

STATION USAGE	NUMBER OF PASSENGERS	LEAST USED
2008/09	204	17
2009/10	252	18
2010/11	248	24
2011/12	260	24
2012/13	170	15
2013/14	314	23

Rawcliffe station is on the Leeds to Goole line four miles west of Goole. It serves the village of Rawcliffe located half a mile away. Although 2013/14 shows an increase in passengers using the station it remains one of the least used stations in Britain.

On 20 August 2009 153317 coupled to a class 150 enter the station with the 18.49 Goole-Leeds.

Britains Least Used Stations 43

PONTEFRACT BAGHILL

OPENED	1 JULY 1879
PRE GROUPING	SWINTON & KNOTTINGLEY JOINT
MANAGED BY	NORTHERN
PLATFORMS	2
REQUEST STOP	NO
SERVICE	MON-FRI SAT SUN
FREQUENCY	C C C

STATION USAGE	NUMBER OF PASSENGERS	LEAST USED
2008/09	3892	162
2009/10	4078	167
2010/11	4308	173
2011/12	5168	178
2012/13	5252	178
2013/14	5666	184

Pontefract Baghill station is situated on a line between Sheffield and York. It only receives two trains in each direction and is the least busy of three Pontefract stations. With an improved service the usage figures would be significantly increased. The other two stations Monkhill and Tanshelf are on the line between Wakefield Kirkdale and Knottingley.

Services are provided by Northern Rail. On 23 April 2013 142015 calls with the 9.29 Sheffield-York.

44   *Britains Least Used Stations*

WENNINGTON

OPENED	2 MAY 1850
PRE GROUPING	MIDLAND
MANAGED BY	NORTHERN
PLATFORMS	2
REQUEST STOP	NO
SERVICE	MON-FRI SAT SUN
FREQUENCY	B B C

STATION USAGE	NUMBER OF PASSENGERS	LEAST USED
2008/09	3040	143
2009/10	3222	146
2010/11	3696	154
2011/12	3340	138
2012/13	2948	132
2013/14	3378	135

Wennington station is situated on the Leeds to Morecambe line 16 miles from Lancaster. It was once a busy junction station with a direct line to Lancaster which closed in 1966.

Northern Rail provide the services which see five trains in each direction on weekdays and four on Sunday. 150273 arrives with the 10.34 Morecambe-Leeds on 20 December 2011.

One service continues to Heysham Port to connect with the sea crossing to the Isle of Man. 150135 approaches Wennington on 20 December 2011 with the 10.19 Leeds-Heysham Port.

Britains Least Used Stations

DENT

OPENED	6 AUGUST 1877
PRE GROUPING	MIDLAND
MANAGED BY	NORTHERN
PLATFORMS	2
REQUEST STOP	NO
SERVICE	MON-FRI SAT SUN
FREQUENCY	B B C

STATION USAGE	NUMBER OF PASSENGERS	LEAST USED
2008/09	8218	244
2009/10	8724	248
2010/11	10558	266
2011/12	10852	255
2012/13	10440	257
2013/14	9742	240

Dent station is on the famous Settle to Carlisle line 17 miles north of Settle. The village of Dent is over four miles from the station. Despite its remote location around 10,000 passengers use the station each year.

At an altitude of 1150 feet above sea level Dent is the highest main line station in England.

The building on the Carlisle bound platform is privately owned and available to rent as holiday accommodation.(right)

Northern Rail provides a service of five or six trains in each direction Monday to Saturday .Three trains each way call on Sunday with an extra Dales Rail service in summer. 153363 coupled to 158645 arrive at Dent on 29 March 2012 with the 11.55 Carlisle- Leeds. (below right)

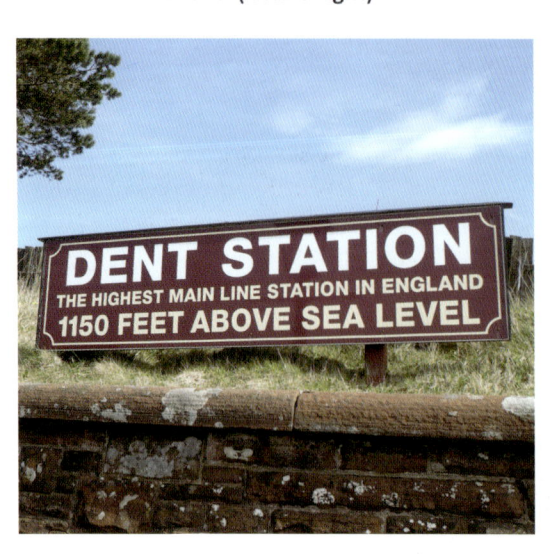

46

Britains Least Used Stations

ULLESKELF

OPENED	30 MAY 1839
PRE GROUPING	NORTH EASTERN
MANAGED BY	NORTHERN
PLATFORMS	2 (ISLAND)
REQUEST STOP	NO
SERVICE	MON-FRI SAT SUN
FREQUENCY	B B X

STATION USAGE	NUMBER OF PASSENGERS	LEAST USED
2008/09	3894	163
2009/10	5102	186
2010/11	6084	199
2011/12	6312	197
2012/13	6420	196
2013/14	7130	206

Ulleskelf station is situated nine miles south west of York on the line to Leeds. The village of Ulleskelf has a population of around 1,000. It is also the nearest station to Tadcaster situated four miles away.

On 23 April 2013 142015 enters Ulleskelf with the 11.05 York-Sheffield.

TransPennine services pass the station at regular intervals. 185113 passes at speed with the 9.50 Middlesbrough-Manchester Airport on 23 April 2013.

Britains Least Used Stations

ARRAM

OPENED	SEPTEMBER 1855
PRE GROUPING	NORTH EASTERN
MANAGED BY	NORTHERN
PLATFORMS	2 (STAGGERED)
REQUEST STOP	NO
SERVICE	MON-FRI SAT SUN
FREQUENCY	B B D

STATION USAGE	NUMBER OF PASSENGERS	LEAST USED
2008/09	2698	134
2009/10	3518	149
2010/11	3234	144
2011/12	3484	141
2012/13	2496	119
2013/14	1900	91

Arram station is situated on the Yorkshire Coast Line between Hull and Scarborough three miles north of Beverley. It serves the small village of Arram with a population of around 200.

Northern Class 158 are employed on the line. 158910 pulls into the station with the 12.44 Hull- Bridlington on 26 February 2014.

Some services continue beyond Hull. 158787 speeds past Arram with the 11.28 Scarborough-Sheffield on 26 February 2014

Britains Least Used Stations

TEESSIDE AIRPORT

OPENED	3 OCTOBER 1971
PRE GROUPING	N/A
MANAGED BY	NORTHERN
PLATFORMS	2
REQUEST STOP	NO
SERVICE	MON-FRI SAT SUN
FREQUENCY	X X E

STATION USAGE	NUMBER OF PASSENGERS	LEAST USED
2008/09	44	1
2009/10	68	2
2010/11	18	1
2011/12	14	1
2012/13	8	1
2013/14	8	1

Teesside Airport station is situated on the Tees Valley Line between Darlington and Middlesbrough. The station is a fifteen minute walk to the Airport Terminal. There are no services on Monday to Saturday and one train in each direction on Sunday. Teesside Airport has been the least used station on the rail network for the past four years with only eight passengers using the station on each of the past two years.
The stations signs show Teesside Airport though National Rail timetables show it as Tees-side Airport.

Northern Rail Class 142 are used on most services on the line. 142015 passes with the 11.35 Darlington-Saltburn on 18 March 2010.

On the same date 142084 is seen working the 11.00 Saltburn-Darlington.

Britains Least Used Stations

SOUTH BANK

OPENED	1 MAY 1882
PRE GROUPING	NORTH EASTERN
MANAGED BY	NORTHERN
PLATFORMS	2 (STAGGERED)
REQUEST STOP	NO
SERVICE	MON-FRI SAT SUN
FREQUENCY	A A A

STATION USAGE	NUMBER OF PASSENGERS	LEAST USED
2008/09	1530	=93
2009/10	1118	67
2010/11	2510	126
2011/12	2654	120
2012/13	4704	168
2013/14	12544	279

South Bank station is situated on The Tees Valley Line two and a half miles east of Middlesbrough. In 1984 the station was resited half a mile west to a more convenient location to serve housing at the south of the station.

With the heavy industrial area in the background 142086 approaches the station with the 12.30 Saltburn-Darlington on 17 August 2013.

South Bank has recently received a much improved service with trains now calling every hour. This has vastly increased the number of passengers using the station. 142023 stands in the platform with the 11.25 Bishop Auckland - Saltburn on 17 August 2013.

Britains Least Used Stations

REDCAR BRITISH STEEL

OPENED	19 JUNE 1978
PRE GROUPING	N/A
MANAGED BY	NORTHERN
PLATFORMS	2
REQUEST STOP	NO
SERVICE	MON-FRI SAT SUN
FREQUENCY	D D X

STATION USAGE	NUMBER OF PASSENGERS	LEAST USED
2008/09	NOT RECORED	
2009/10	1560	83
2010/11	954	57
2011/12	822	51
2012/13	890	52
2013/14	1418	70

Redcar British Steel station is on the Darlington to Saltburn line two miles west of Redcar Central. The station is situated on the Teesside Steelworks site and there is no public access to the station.

Redcar British Steel receives one train in each direction for workers at the steel works. 142084 calls with the 16.30 Saltburn-Bishop Auckland on 13 June 2014.

With part of the steelworks seen in the background 142084 passes with the 15.30 Darlington- Saltburn on 13 June 2014.

Britains Least Used Stations

51

GREAT AYTON

OPENED	1 APRIL 1868
PRE GROUPING	NORTH EASTERN
MANAGED BY	NORTHERN
PLATFORMS	1
REQUEST STOP	NO
SERVICE	MON-FRI SAT SUN
FREQUENCY	C C C

STATION USAGE	NUMBER OF PASSENGERS	LEAST USED
2008/09	5650	203
2009/10	6134	206
2010/11	6798	211
2011/12	6904	205
2012/13	5738	191
2013/14	6826	198

Great Ayton station is on the Esk Valley Line between Middlesbrough and Whitby eight and a half miles south east of Middlesbrough. It serves the village of Great Ayton located one mile from the station.

The line has a service of four trains in each direction including Sunday. 156443 enters the station with the 14.16 Middlesbrough-Whitby on 14 April 2009.

Northern Rail Class 156 DMUs are used on the line. 156469 approaches Great Ayton on 13 June 2014 with the 12.18 Whitby-Middlesbrough.

Britains Least Used Stations

BATTERSBY

OPENED	1 APRIL 1868
PRE GROUPING	NORTH EASTERN
MANAGED BY	NORTHERN
PLATFORMS	1
REQUEST STOP	NO
SERVICE	MON-FRI SAT SUN
FREQUENCY	C C C

STATION USAGE	NUMBER OF PASSENGERS	LEAST USED
2008/09	1806	104
2009/10	2012	111
2010/11	1476	76
2011/12	1504	80
2012/13	1574	75
2013/14	1592	77

Battersby station is on the line between Middlesbrough and Whitby. It serves a tiny hamlet and is the least used station on the line.

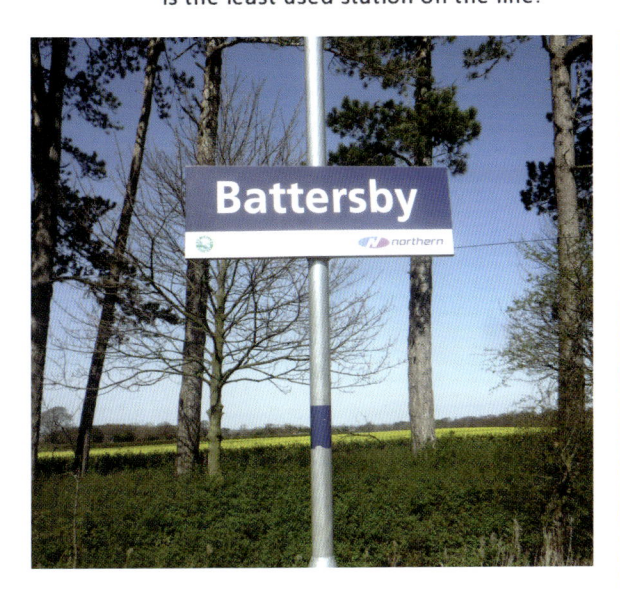

A line used to run from Battersby to join the East Coast Main Line at Northallerton but this line was closed in 1954.

Trains have to reverse at Battersby. 156444 has just arrived with the 16.00 Whitby-Middlesbrough on 15 April 2014. The driver is seen changing ends to take the train forward to Middlesbrough.

Britains Least Used Stations 53

KILDALE

OPENED	1 APRIL 1861
PRE GROUPING	NORTH EASTERN
MANAGED BY	NORTHERN
PLATFORMS	1
REQUEST STOP	NO
SERVICE FREQUENCY	MON-FRI SAT SUN C C C

STATION USAGE	NUMBER OF PASSENGERS	LEAST USED
2008/09	2308	123
2009/10	2006	=109
2010/11	1992	103
2011/12	2018	102
2012/13	1822	91
2013/14	1960	94

Kildale station is on the Middlesbrough to Whitby Line thirteen miles from Middlesbrough. The small village of Kildale is situated within the North York Moors National Park on the Cleveland Way National Trail.

Stations on the Esk Valley Line are well cared for with plenty of flowers on display.

156444 enters Kildale with the 14.14 Middlesbrough – Whitby service on 15 April 2014.

54   Britains Least Used Stations

COMMONDALE

OPENED	DECEMBER 1882
PRE GROUPING	NORTH EASTERN
MANAGED BY	NORTHERN
PLATFORMS	1
REQUEST STOP	NO
SERVICE	MON-FRI SAT SUN
FREQUENCY	C C C

STATION USAGE	NUMBER OF PASSENGERS	LEAST USED
2008/09	3142	148
2009/10	2858	139
2010/11	3972	162
2011/12	5000	173
2012/13	4852	171
2013/14	5026	175

Commondale station is on the Esk Valley Line half way between Middlesbrough and Whitby. The village of Commondale with a population of around 130 is situated half a mile from the station.

The station can only be reached by using a footpath across a field.

156444 is seen arriving on 15 April 2014 with the 16.00 Whitby-Middlesbrough.

Britains Least Used Stations

CASTLETON MOOR

OPENED	1 APRIL 1861
PRE GROUPING	NORTH EASTERN
MANAGED BY	NORTHERN
PLATFORMS	1
REQUEST STOP	NO
SERVICE	MON-FRI SAT SUN
FREQUENCY	C C C

STATION USAGE	NUMBER OF PASSENGERS	LEAST USED
2008/09	5172	193
2009/10	5544	196
2010/11	5164	189
2011/12	5030	174
2012/13	4850	170
2013/14	4892	=170

Castleton Moor station is on the Middlesbrough to Whitby line 18 miles from Middlesbrough. The station serves the village of Castleton. Located in the North York Moors it is a popular destination for walkers.

Two views of 156443 first arriving at Castleton Moor and second ready to depart with the 12.41 Whitby Middlesbrough on 14 April 2009.

Britains Least Used Stations

SLEIGHTS

OPENED	MAY 1848
PRE GROUPING	NORTH EASTERN
MANAGED BY	NORTHERN
PLATFORMS	1
REQUEST STOP	NO
SERVICE	MON-FRI SAT SUN
FREQUENCY	C C C

STATION USAGE	NUMBER OF PASSENGERS	LEAST USED
2008/09	3884	161
2009/10	4334	174
2010/11	4292	172
2011/12	4592	168
2012/13	4378	161
2013/14	4426	157

Sleights station is on the Esk Valley Line three miles from Whitby. The station serves the village of Sleights. It is one of the best cared for stations on the line with plenty of flowers and plants on display. The station building is in private ownership.

156444 pauses at Sleights on 15 April 2014 with the 10.36 Middlesbrough-Whitby.

The same unit is approaching the station with the 12.41 Whitby- Middlesbrough.

Britains Least Used Stations 57

RUSWARP

OPENED	MAY 1848
PRE GROUPING	NORTH EASTERN
MANAGED BY	NORTHERN
PLATFORMS	1
REQUEST STOP	NO
SERVICE	MON-FRI SAT SUN
FREQUENCY	C C C

STATION USAGE	NUMBER OF PASSENGERS	LEAST USED
2008/09	3054	145
2009/10	2606	131
2010/11	2722	133
2011/12	2974	130
2012/13	2946	131
2013/14	3032	125

Ruswarp is the final intermediate station on the Esk Valley Line one and a half miles from Whitby. The station serves the village of Ruswarp which is located on the River Esk.

On 18 May 2010 Northern Class 156 no 156490 is ready to leave with the 12.41 Whitby-Middlesbrough.

BLAYDON

OPENED	10 MARCH 1835
PRE GROUPING	NORTH EASTERN
MANAGED BY	NORTHERN
PLATFORMS	2
REQUEST STOP	NO
SERVICE	MON-FRI SAT SUN
FREQUENCY	B B B

STATION USAGE	NUMBER OF PASSENGERS	LEAST USED
2008/09	3828	158
2009/10	2752	137
2010/11	4284	171
2011/12	4220	158
2012/13	2770	126
2013/14	5002	174

Blaydon station is situated on the Tyne Valley Line between Newcastle and Carlisle five and a half miles from Newcastle. Blaydon has had a poor service of three trains in each direction which accounts for its low usage for a town of its size. However since December 2013 the service has increased to a train every two hours.

Northern Classes 142 and 156 provide services on the line. 156475 runs past Blaydon with the 13.30 Carlisle-Newcastle on 28 August 2013.

On the same date 142090 is seen from the footbridge with the 13.32 Middlesbrough-Hexham.

Britains Least Used Stations

DUNSTON

OPENED	1 JANUARY 1909
PRE GROUPING	NORTH EASTERN
MANAGED BY	NORTHERN
PLATFORMS	2 (ISLAND)
REQUEST STOP	NO
SERVICE	MON-FRI SAT SUN
FREQUENCY	B B B

STATION USAGE	NUMBER OF PASSENGERS	LEAST USED
2008/09	2896	140
2009/10	2312	123
2010/11	2248	113
2011/12	2664	122
2012/13	2164	102
2013/14	2336	108

Dunston station is situated on the Newcastle to Carlisle line just over two miles from Newcastle. The station was opened as Dunston-on-Tyne. It was closed in 1926 and reopened in 1984 as Dunston.

A view from the entrance looking towards Newcastle.

Dunston like Blaydon has received a much improved service since December 2013. 156443 departs with the 17.44 Newcastle-Metro Centre on 28 August 2013.

60   Britains Least Used Stations

MANORS

OPENED	1 JULY 1847
PRE GROUPING	NORTH EASTERN
MANAGED BY	NORTHERN
PLATFORMS	2 (ISLAND)
REQUEST STOP	NO
SERVICE	MON-FRI SAT SUN
FREQUENCY	A A X

STATION USAGE	NUMBER OF PASSENGERS	LEAST USED
2008/09	2574	132
2009/10	2998	143
2010/11	2976	137
2011/12	4120	156
2012/13	3872	152
2013/14	4444	158

Manors station is situated half a mile north of Newcastle on the East Coast Main Line. Between 1909 and 1969 the station was known as Manors East. The low number of passengers using the station is partly due to the Tyne and Wear Metro station more conveniently located 100 yards away.

Most services to call at Manors originate from Morpeth. 142019 is seen with the 16.49 Morpeth-Newcastle on 28 August 2013.

HST No 43311 with 43208 at the rear has just left Newcastle with the 14.00 Kings Cross-Aberdeen on 28 August 2013.

Britains Least Used Stations 61

PEGSWOOD

OPENED	JANUARY 1903
PRE GROUPING	NORTH EASTERN
MANAGED BY	NORTHERN
PLATFORMS	2
REQUEST STOP	NO
SERVICE	MON-FRI SAT SUN
FREQUENCY	D D X

STATION USAGE	NUMBER OF PASSENGERS	LEAST USED
2008/09	2788	136
2009/10	2688	135
2010/11	1102	64
2011/12	1900	96
2012/13	1650	80
2013/14	1166	57

Pegswood station is situated on the East Coast Main Line between Newcastle and Edinburgh two miles north of Morpeth. It receives a limited service of one morning and one evening train to Chathill and one in the morning to Newcastle.

East Coast services north of Newcastle run every hour to Edinburgh with some continuing to Glasgow or Aberdeen. 91124 approaches Pegswood at speed with the 8.00 Kings Cross-Edinburgh on 3 August 2010.

On the same date a Class 220 Voyager rushes through the station with the 9.00 Glasgow Central-Penzance Cross Country service.

Britains Least Used Stations

WIDDRINGTON

OPENED	1 JULY 1847
PRE GROUPING	NORTH EASTERN
MANAGED BY	NORTHERN
PLATFORMS	2
REQUEST STOP	NO
SERVICE	MON-FRI SAT SUN
FREQUENCY	D D X

STATION USAGE	NUMBER OF PASSENGERS	LEAST USED
2008/09	6314	218
2009/10	6398	213
2010/11	5124	188
2011/12	5268	180
2012/13	3630	147
2013/14	4962	172

Widdrington station is on the East Coast Main Line 23 miles north of Newcastle. The station serves a village called Widdrington Station and a separate village called Widdrington one mile away. The station receives the same service as Pegswood.

A class 220 Voyager passes Widdrington on 3 August 2010 with the 6.27 Bristol Temple Meads-Edinburgh.

Taken from the same spot a Class 91 is seen speeding through the station with the 9.00 Kings Cross-Edinburgh.

Britains Least Used Stations 63

ACKLINGTON

OPENED	1 JULY 1847
PRE GROUPING	NORTH EASTERN
MANAGED BY	NORTHERN
PLATFORMS	2
REQUEST STOP	NO
SERVICE	MON-FRI SAT SUN
FREQUENCY	D D X

STATION USAGE	NUMBER OF PASSENGERS	LEAST USED
2008/09	778	53
2009/10	268	=19
2010/11	108	13
2011/12	192	17
2012/13	184	16
2013/14	176	16

Acklington station is on the East Coast Main Line 28 miles north of Newcastle. The station serves the small village of Acklington located half a mile from the station. Around 200 passengers use the station each year making it one of the least used on the rail network.

On 3 August 2010 a Class 221 Voyager passes at speed with the 6.25 Plymouth-Edinburgh Cross Country service.

On the same date a HST is seen hurrying through Acklington with the 10.30 Kings Cross – Aberdeen.

Britains Least Used Stations

CHATHILL

OPENED	29 MARCH 1847
PRE GROUPING	NORTH EASTERN
MANAGED BY	NORTHERN
PLATFORMS	2
REQUEST STOP	NO
SERVICE	MON-FRI SAT SUN
FREQUENCY	D D X

STATION USAGE	NUMBER OF PASSENGERS	LEAST USED
2008/09	1864	107
2009/10	2612	132
2010/11	2642	130
2011/12	5250	179
2012/13	2794	128
2013/14	2578	115

Chathill station is situated on the East Coast Main Line 46 miles north of Newcastle and 22 miles from the Scottish border. It is the northern terminus for the morning and afternoon commuter services to and from Newcastle. The station serves several small villages including Chathill.

Chathill is one of the best kept stations in the country. The station house is surrounded by tubs and hanging baskets containing colourful flowers and plants.

Britains Least Used Stations

65

CHATHILL

Services are provided by Northern Rail. On 16 August 2011 156463 has just arrived with the 17.01 Newcastle-Chathill. The unit will now run northbound for five miles to Belford loop to change tracks for the return working.

156463 has returned to Chathill to form the 19.08 Chathill-Hexham (via Newcastle).

PEARTREE

OPENED	12 AUGUST 1839
PRE GROUPING	MIDLAND
MANAGED BY	EAST MIDLANDS
PLATFORMS	2
REQUEST STOP	NO
SERVICE	MON-FRI SAT SUN
FREQUENCY	C C X

STATION USAGE	NUMBER OF PASSENGERS	LEAST USED
2008/09	1678	101
2009/10	2810	138
2010/11	2274	115
2011/12	2756	125
2012/13	3234	136
2013/14	4154	150

Peartree station is situated just over one mile from Derby on the line to Birmingham and Crewe. The station serves the Peartree and Normanton districts of Derby. The station was opened as Pear Tree (two words) and Normanton. It was closed in 1968 and reopened in 1976 as Peartree.

The station is served by a limited service operated by East Midlands Trains between Derby and Crewe. 153319 calls with the 16.40 Derby-Crewe on 14 May 2009.

Taken from the bridge at the south of the station a Class 221 Voyager is seen passing on 26 March 2014 with the 11.00 Glasgow Central-Penzance.

Britains Least Used Stations 67

KEMPSTON HARDWICK

OPENED	30 OCTOBER 1905
PRE GROUPING	LONDON & NORTH WESTERN
MANAGED BY	LONDON MIDLAND
PLATFORMS	2
REQUEST STOP	NO
SERVICE	MON-FRI SAT SUN
FREQUENCY	A A X

STATION USAGE	NUMBER OF PASSENGERS	LEAST USED
2008/09	8252	245
2009/10	6350	210
2010/11	6284	204
2011/12	7316	209
2012/13	5626	187
2013/14	7032	203

Kempston Hardwick station is one of ten intermediate stations on the Marston Vale Line between Bedford and Bletchley. It is situated four miles from Bedford and serves the small village of Kempston Hardwick.

Kempston Hardwick is the least used station on the line. Services are provided by London Midland. On 4 September 2012 153364 calls with the 15.55 Bedford -Bletchley.

On the same date 150107 arrives at Kempston Hardwick with the 15.47 Bletchley-Bedford. (note the incorrect destination on the train)

Britains Least Used Stations

POLESWORTH

OPENED	15 SEPTEMBER 1847
PRE GROUPING	LONDON & NORTH WESTERN
MANAGED BY	LONDON MIDLAND
PLATFORMS	2 (ONE NOT IN USE)
REQUEST STOP	NO
SERVICE	MON-FRI SAT SUN
FREQUENCY	D D X

STATION USAGE	NUMBER OF PASSENGERS	LEAST USED
2008/09	216	=19
2009/10	276	22
2010/11	690	47
2011/12	1374	72
2012/13	722	46
2013/14	702	41

Polesworth station is on the Trent Valley section of the West Coast Main Line three and a half miles south of Tamworth. In 2005 following modernisation to the West Coast Main Line the footbridge to the up platform was never replaced. This means trains can only call on northbound services.

A southbound Pendolino speeds past the disused platform on 8 April 2014.(right)

Polesworth now receives just one northbound service Monday to Saturday provided by London Midland. 350109 passes the station with the 10.46 Euston-Crewe on 8 April 2014. (below)

When the station had a more frequent service 350122 picks up passengers on the 13.47 Rugby-Crewe service on 17 February 2006. (below right)

Britains Least Used Stations   69

NORTON BRIDGE

OPENED	4 JULY 1837
PRE GROUPING	LONDON & NORTH WESTERN
MANAGED BY	LONDON MIDLAND
PLATFORMS	2 (ISLAND)
REQUEST STOP	NO
SERVICE	MON-FRI SAT SUN
FREQUENCY	B B X
STATION USAGE	NUMBER OF PASSENGERS LEAST USED
2008/09	N/A
2009/10	N/A
2010/11	N/A
2011/12	N/A
2012/13	N/A
2013/14	N/A

Norton Bridge station is on the West Coast Main Line four miles north of Stafford. The main line platforms were removed in the 1960's when electrification took place. In 2004 after upgrading of the line the footbridge to the remaining island platform was removed. As a result train services have been replaced by buses between Stone and Stafford.

A Cross Country Voyager heads south with the 11.27 Manchester Piccadilly-Bournemouth on 13 April 2010.

On the same day a Class 350 Desiro is seen passing with the 10.36 Birmingham New Street-Liverpool Lime Street.

Britains Least Used Stations

BARLASTON

OPENED	17 APRIL 1848
PRE GROUPING	NORTH STAFFORDSHIRE
MANAGED BY	LONDON MIDLAND
PLATFORMS	2
REQUEST STOP	NO
SERVICE FREQUENCY	MON-FRI SAT SUN B B X

STATION USAGE	NUMBER OF PASSENGERS	LEAST USED
2008/09	N/A	
2009/10	N/A	
2010/11	N/A	
2011/12	N/A	
2012/13	N/A	
2013/14	N/A	

Barlaston station is situated on the line between Manchester and Stafford five miles south of Stoke on Trent. The station was originally known as Barlaston and Tittensor and became Barlaston in 1972.

Since 2004 trains have been replaced by buses which run between Stoke and Stone.

A Pendolino hurries through Barlaston with the 9.15 Manchester Piccadilly-Euston on 13 April 2010.

On the same date 350118 heads north with the 7.46 Euston-Crewe.

Britains Least Used Stations

71

WEDGWOOD

OPENED	1 JANUARY 1940
PRE GROUPING	N/A
MANAGED BY	LONDON MIDLAND
PLATFORMS	2
REQUEST STOP	NO
SERVICE	MON-FRI SAT SUN
FREQUENCY	B B X

STATION USAGE	NUMBER OF PASSENGERS	LEAST USED
2008/09	N/A	
2009/10	N/A	
2010/11	N/A	
2011/12	N/A	
2012/13	N/A	
2013/14	N/A	

Wedgwood station is situated on the line between Manchester and Stafford four miles south of Stoke on Trent. The station was originally opened for employees of the pottery firm J Wedgwood and sons. Like Barlaston and Norton Bridge the station is served by buses.

A Pendolino approaches the station past the automated level crossing with the 10.15 Manchester Piccadilly-Euston on 13 August 2010.

On the same date 350122 heads towards Stoke with the 8.46 Euston - Crewe.

Britains Least Used Stations

DOVEY JUNCTION

OPENED	14 AUGUST 1867
PRE GROUPING	CAMBRIAN
MANAGED BY	ARRIVA TRAINS WALES
PLATFORMS	2
REQUEST STOP	NO
SERVICE	MON-FRI SAT SUN
FREQUENCY	B B D

STATION USAGE	NUMBER OF PASSENGERS	LEAST USED
2008/09	1494	91
2009/10	1768	95
2010/11	1482	77
2011/12	1288	66
2012/13	1694	83
2013/14	1828	87

Dovey Junction station is on the Cambrian Coast Line four miles west of Machynlleth. It is where the line splits into the line to Aberystwyth and the Cambrian Coast Line to Pwllheli. The only access to the station is a three quarter mile path from the end of the Aberystwyth platform which leads to the hamlet of Glandyfi.

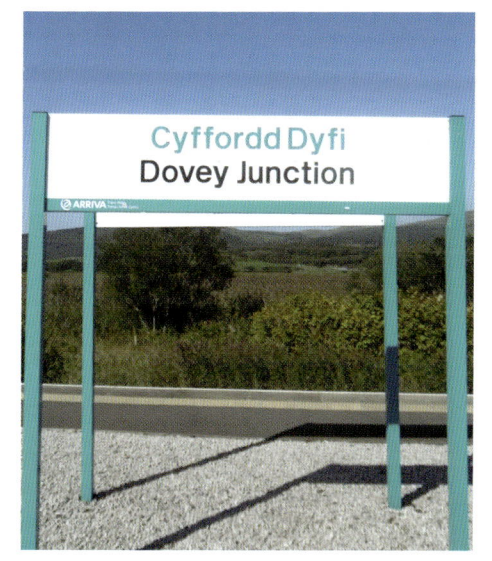

Having split with a Pwllheli service at Machynlleth 158824 is ready to leave with the 8.08 Birmingham International -Aberystwyth on 2 September 2014.

On 24 April 2009 158837 is seen departing Dovey Junction with the 11.38 Pwllheli-Birmingham International. This service will join a service from Aberystwyth at Machynlleth. The Aberystwyth platform is seen to the left of the picture.

Britains Least Used Stations

TONFANAU

OPENED	JULY 1896
PRE GROUPING	CAMBRIAN
MANAGED BY	ARRIVA TRAINS WALES
PLATFORMS	1
REQUEST STOP	YES
SERVICE	MON-FRI SAT SUN
FREQUENCY	B B D

STATION USAGE	NUMBER OF PASSENGERS	LEAST USED
2008/09	1352	86
2009/10	3016	144
2010/11	2726	134
2011/12	2150	107
2012/13	2240	107
2013/14	2728	118

Tonfanau station is on the Cambrian Coast Line nine and a half miles south of Barmouth. It is in a remote location near the coast with very few houses nearby. In 1996 the station was upgraded with a new platform, signage and lighting.

All services on the line are provided by Arriva Trains Wales. 158837 pauses with the 9.05 Machynlleth-Pwllheli on 24 April 2009.

On the same date 158833 departs Tonfanau with the 7.28 Pwllheli-Birmingham International.

74   Britains Least Used Stations

LLANABER

OPENED	JULY 1914
PRE GROUPING	CAMBRIAN
MANAGED BY	ARRIVA TRAINS WALES
PLATFORMS	1
REQUEST STOP	YES
SERVICE FREQUENCY	MON-FRI SAT SUN B B D

STATION USAGE	NUMBER OF PASSENGERS	LEAST USED
2008/09	3766	156
2009/10	4818	182
2010/11	3140	141
2011/12	2496	117
2012/13	3928	=153
2013/14	2238	=106

Llanaber station is on the Cambrian Coast Line just over one mile north of Barmouth. The station is located on a narrow ledge below the village and above the beach. In January 2014 storm damage north of the station closed the line for four months.

The proximity to the sea can be seen in this view of 158835 approaching Llanaber with the 13.42 Pwllheli-Birmingham International on 23 April 2009.

Britains Least Used Stations

PENSARN

OPENED	10 OCTOBER 1867
PRE GROUPING	CAMBRIAN
MANAGED BY	ARRIVA TRAINS WALES
PLATFORMS	1
REQUEST STOP	YES
SERVICE	MON-FRI SAT SUN
FREQUENCY	B B D

STATION USAGE	NUMBER OF PASSENGERS	LEAST USED
2008/09	2806	137
2009/10	2730	136
2010/11	2084	106
2011/12	2016	101
2012/13	2362	116
2013/14	1810	86

Pensarn station is situated on the Cambrian Coast Line eight miles north of Barmouth. The station opened as Llanbedr and Pensarn. In 1978 it became Pensarn when a station three quarter of a mile to the south changed its name from Talwrn Bach to Llanbedr.

The Cambrian Coast Line has a two hourly service on weekdays . 158835 pauses with the 11.00 Machynlleth-Pwllheli on 23 April 2009.

On 2 September 2014 158831 is ready to leave with the 15.37 Pwllheli-Birmingham International.

76 Britains Least Used Stations

LLANDANWG

OPENED	8 NOVEMBER 1929
PRE GROUPING	CAMBRIAN
MANAGED BY	ARRIVA TRAINS WALES
PLATFORMS	1
REQUEST STOP	YES
SERVICE	MON-FRI SAT SUN
FREQUENCY	B B D

STATION USAGE	NUMBER OF PASSENGERS	LEAST USED
2008/09	3858	160
2009/10	5304	189
2010/11	4756	181
2011/12	5634	186
2012/13	5466	189
2013/14	4382	=154

Llandanwg station is on the Cambrian Coast Line two miles south of Harlech. The station serves the village of Llandanwg. The small blue waiting shelter is typical of many stations on the line.

158835 calls with the 11.00 Machynlleth -Pwllheli on 23 April 2009.

On 2 September 2014 the same unit is seen again approaching Llandanwg with the 17.45 Pwllheli-Machynlleth.

Britains Least Used Stations

TYGWYN

OPENED	11 JULY 1927
PRE GROUPING	CAMBRIAN
MANAGED BY	ARRIVA TRAINS WALES
PLATFORMS	1
REQUEST STOP	YES
SERVICE	MON-FRI SAT SUN
FREQUENCY	B B D

STATION USAGE	NUMBER OF PASSENGERS	LEAST USED
2008/09	1112	70
2009/10	2072	114
2010/11	2048	104
2011/12	1418	=73
2012/13	1938	94
2013/14	1364	66

Tygwyn station is on the Cambrian Coast Line three miles north of Harlech. The station is located where the line crosses the A 496 road between Harlech and Talsarnu. There are very few houses nearby.

On 23 April 2009 158835 pauses at the short platform with the 11.00 Machynlleth-Pwllheli.

On 2 September 2014 158831 is seen arriving with the 10.08 Birmingham International-Pwllheli.

Britains Least Used Stations

LLANDECWYN

OPENED	18 NOVEMBER 1935
PRE GROUPING	N/A
MANAGED BY	ARRIVA TRAINS WALES
PLATFORMS	1
REQUEST STOP	YES
SERVICE	MON-FRI SAT SUN
FREQUENCY	B B D

STATION USAGE	NUMBER OF PASSENGERS	LEAST USED
2008/09	1474	90
2009/10	1812	100
2010/11	1906	=97
2011/12	1418	=73
2012/13	998	56
2013/14	880	48

Llandecwyn station is on the Cambrian Coast Line five miles north of Harlech. The station is situated on the estuary of the Afon Dwyryd. With fewer than 1,000 passengers Llandecwyn is the least used station on the Cambrian Coast Line.

The Afon Dwyryd estuary is seen to the right of the picture as 158835 pauses in the short platform with the 11.00 Machynlleth- Pwllheli service on 23 April 2009.

Following the severe floods in early 2014 the station was completely rebuilt. 158825 forming the 15.37 Pwllheli-Birmingham International is seen approaching the rebuilt platform on 2 September 2014, the second day after its reopening.

Britains Least Used Stations 79

PENYCHAIN

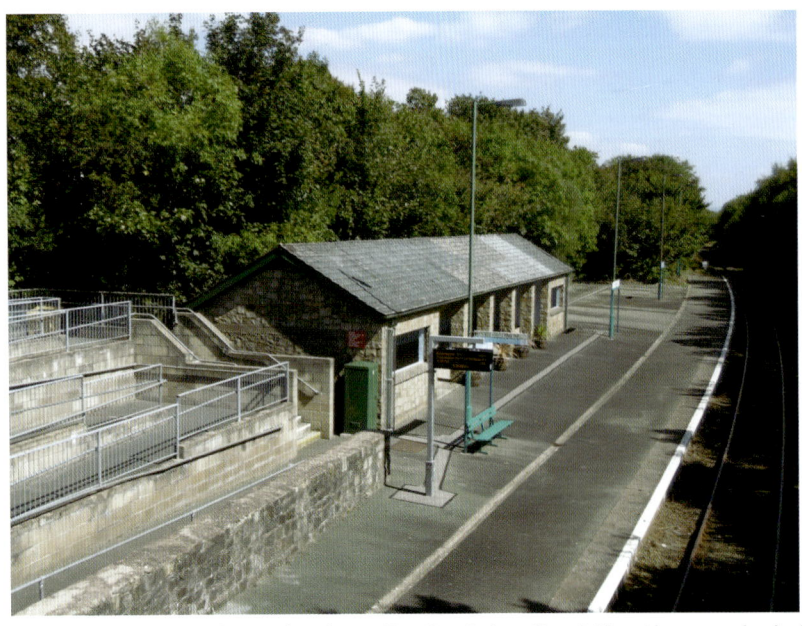

OPENED	31 JULY 1933
PRE GROUPING	N/A
MANAGED BY	ARRIVA TRAINS WALES
PLATFORMS	1
REQUEST STOP	YES
SERVICE	MON-FRI SAT SUN
FREQUENCY	B B D

STATION USAGE	NUMBER OF PASSENGERS	LEAST USED
2008/09	1896	110
2009/10	2446	127
2010/11	2394	122
2011/12	3060	135
2012/13	3252	137
2013/14	3276	133

Penychain station is on the Cambrian Coast Line three and a half miles from the terminus at Pwllheli. It was originally known as Butlins Penychain and became Penychain in 2001. The station used to serve Butlins Holiday Camp and was particularly busy in the 1950s and early 1960s. The station now serves the Haven Holiday Park situated on the site of the old Butlins Holiday Camp.

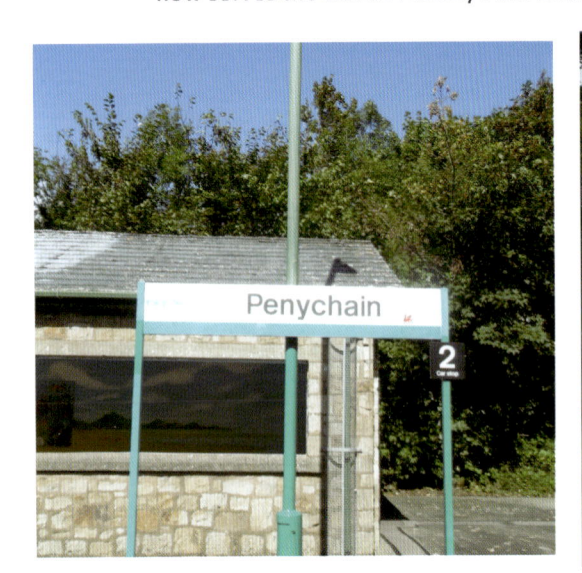

158835 Calls with the 11.00 Machynlleth-Pwllheli on 23 April 2009.

158825 is seen arriving at Penychain with the 13.38 Pwllheli-Birmingham International on 2 September 2014.

Britains Least Used Stations

ABERERCH

OPENED	10 OCTOBER 1867
PRE GROUPING	CAMBRIAN
MANAGED BY	ARRIVA TRAINS WALES
PLATFORMS	1
REQUEST STOP	YES
SERVICE	MON-FRI SAT SUN
FREQUENCY	B B D

STATION USAGE	NUMBER OF PASSENGERS	LEAST USED
2008/09	1258	83
2009/10	1326	73
2010/11	1620	82
2011/12	1786	90
2012/13	1214	64
2013/14	1380	67

Abererch station is on the Cambrian Coast Line two miles east of the terminus at Pwllheli. The station is located between the village of Abererch and the beach.

On 23 April 2009 158835 makes its final call at Abererch with the 11.00 from Machynlleth to Pwllheli.

158825 is seen departing Abererch on 2 September 2014 with the 8.08 service from Birmingham International.

Britains Least Used Stations

ARDWICK

OPENED	NOVEMBER 1842
PRE GROUPING	GREAT CENTRAL
MANAGED BY	NORTHERN
PLATFORMS	2 (ISLAND)
REQUEST STOP	NO
SERVICE	MON-FRI SAT SUN
FREQUENCY	C X X

STATION USAGE	NUMBER OF PASSENGERS	LEAST USED
2008/09	574	45
2009/10	754	53
2010/11	668	46
2011/12	584	40
2012/13	616	39
2013/14	568	35

Ardwick station is half a mile from Manchester Piccadilly on the line to Hadfield and on TransPennine routes to the north east. The station is situated in an industrial area of the city and receives only a peak hour service operated by Northern.

On 20 September 2013 323234 heads towards Manchester Piccadilly with the 11.00 service from Hadfield. A Cross Country Voyager can be seen on the Manchester branch of the West Coast Main Line.

170307 runs through Ardwick on 27 March 2007 with the 10.42 Manchester Piccadilly-Hull.

82 Britains Least Used Stations

REDDISH SOUTH

OPENED	JULY 1859
PRE GROUPING	LONDON & NORTH WESTERN
MANAGED BY	NORTHERN
PLATFORMS	1
REQUEST STOP	YES
SERVICE	MON-FRI SAT SUN
FREQUENCY	E X X

STATION USEAGE	NUMBER OF PASSENGERS	LEAST USED
2008/09	274	27
2009/10	76	3
2010/11	68	=5
2011/12	56	4
2012/13	122	10
2013/14	26	3

Reddish South station is on the line between Stockport and Guide Bridge south east of Manchester. The station originally had two island platforms. Now only one run down platform remains with no facilities or lighting. Reddish North station is half a mile away and has a regular service into Manchester Piccadilly.

Reddish South receives one train per week on a Friday morning on a service between Stockport and Stalybridge. With such a poor service it is not surprising that it is one of the least used stations on the rail network.

The service is provided by Northern Rail using Class 142 DMUs. On 20 September 2013 142035/049 enter the station with the 10.13 Stockport-Stalybridge.

Britains Least Used Stations

DENTON

OPENED	FEBRUARY 1851
PRE GROUPING	LONDON & NORTH WESTERN
MANAGED BY	NORTHERN
PLATFORMS	2
REQUEST STOP	YES
SERVICE	MON-FRI SAT SUN
FREQUENCY	E X X

STATION USAGE	NUMBER OF PASSENGERS	LEAST USED
2008/09	56	2
2009/10	496	41
2010/11	52	4
2011/12	30	3
2012/13	194	18
2013/14	110	10

Denton station is on the line between Stockport and Guide Bridge, south east of Manchester. It still retains an island platform but like Reddish South receives just one train per week.

142037/031 enter the station with the 9.22 Stockport-Guide Bridge on 27 March 2009. Two Class 142 units are used on this service.

142035/049 depart Denton with the 10.13 Stockport-Stalybridge on 20 September 2013.

84   *Britains Least Used Stations*

BODORGAN

OPENED	OCTOBER 1849
PRE GROUPING	LONDON & NORTH WESTERN
MANAGED BY	ARRIVA TRAINS WALES
PLATFORMS	2
REQUEST STOP	YES
SERVICE FREQUENCY	MON-FRI SAT SUN B B C

STATION USAGE	NUMBER OF PASSENGERS	LEAST USED
2008/09	3966	167
2009/10	5354	190
2010/11	7314	223
2011/12	8406	228
2012/13	7736	221
2013/14	5638	183

Bodorgan station is on the North Wales Coast Line on the Isle of Anglesey. It is 12 miles from Holyhead. and serves the villages of Bodorgan and Bethel on the south of the Island.

Bodorgan receives a two hourly service on weekdays with five in each direction on Sunday. Services are provided by Arriva Trains Wales. 158819 calls with the 11.23 Holyhead-Birmingham New Street on 21 April 2009.

Some services continue to South Wales via Chester and Shrewsbury. 175108 is seen passing with the 12.38 Holyhead-Maesteg on 21 April 2009.

Britains Least Used Stations 85

TY CROES

OPENED	NOVEMBER 1848
PRE GROUPING	LONDON & NORTH WESTERN
MANAGED BY	ARRIVA TRAINS WALES
PLATFORMS	2 (STAGGERED)
REQUEST STOP	YES
SERVICE FREQUENCY	MON-FRI SAT SUN B B C

STATION USAGE	NUMBER OF PASSENGERS	LEAST USED
2008/09	4164	173
2009/10	3732	155
2010/11	4612	178
2011/12	3718	148
2012/13	4066	158
2013/14	4142	149

Ty Croes is one of six stations on Anglesey and is situated nine miles from Holyhead on the south side of the island.

The station is served by Arriva Trains Wales and like Bodorgan receives a two hourly service on weekdays with five in each direction on Sunday. 158839 is seen entering the station with the 13.23 Holyhead-Birmingham International on 21 March 2009.

A view showing the signal box and level crossing separating the staggered platforms as a Virgin Voyager heads towards Holyhead on 21 March 2009 with the 9.10 service from Euston.

CLIFTON

OPENED	JUNE 1847
PRE GROUPING	LANCASHIRE & YORKSHIRE
MANAGED BY	NORTHERN
PLATFORMS	2
REQUEST STOP	NO
SERVICE	MON-FRI SAT SUN
FREQUENCY	D D X

STATION USAGE	NUMBER OF PASSENGERS	LEAST USED
2008/09	216	=19
2009/10	278	23
2010/11	170	16
2011/12	496	38
2012/13	334	27
2013/14	298	22

Clifton station is situated on the line between Bolton and Manchester just under five miles from Manchester Victoria. The station opened as Clifton Junction and became Clifton in 1974.

Clifton receives one morning service to Manchester and one afternoon service to Wigan operated by Northern. 150223 runs through the station with the 7.22 Wigan Wallgate-Manchester Victoria on 26 March 2014.

142011 is seen heading north with the 7.06 Manchester Victoria-Southport on 24 March 2009.

Britains Least Used Stations 87

HOSCAR

OPENED	1 NOVEMBER 1870
PRE GROUPING	LANCASHIRE & YORKSHIRE
MANAGED BY	NORTHERN
PLATFORMS	2 (STAGGERED)
REQUEST STOP	NO
SERVICE FREQUENCY	MON-FRI SAT SUN B B X

STATION USAGE	NUMBER OF PASSENGERS	LEAST USED
2008/09	1530	=93
2009/10	1268	71
2010/11	1552	80
2011/12	1202	63
2012/13	1600	77
2013/14	1436	72

Hoscar station is on the Manchester to Southport line eight miles west of Wigan Wallgate. It was known as Hoscar Moss until 1900. The station serves the hamlet of Hoscar and the village of Lathom.

150245 is seen passing the level crossing which separate the platforms with the 11.38 Southport - Manchester Airport on 18 November 2008.

The station is served by Northern Rail and has a service every two hours. 142014/032 enter the station with the 9.51 Southport-Manchester Victoria on 6 June 2015.

88 Britains Least Used Stations

NEW LANE

OPENED	9 APRIL 1855
PRE GROUPING	LANCASHIRE & YORKSHIRE
MANAGED BY	NORTHERN
PLATFORMS	2 (STAGGERED)
REQUEST STOP	NO
SERVICE FREQUENCY	MON-FRI SAT SUN B B X

STATION USAGE	NUMBER OF PASSENGERS	LEAST USED
2008/09	3110	146
2009/10	2674	134
2010/11	3034	139
2011/12	3280	137
2012/13	3312	139
2013/14	3030	124

New Lane station is situated on the Manchester to Southport line just over one mile west of Burscough Bridge station. It serves several small hamlets and farming communities and is one mile from Martin Mere Bird Sanctuary.

142052 approaches the station over the level crossing with the 9.46 Manchester Victoria-Southport on 24 September 2013.

On the same date 150270/142058 pass New Lane with the 10.24 Southport - Manchester Airport.

Britains Least Used Stations

BESCAR LANE

OPENED	9 APRIL 1855
PRE GROUPING	LANCASHIRE & YORKSHIRE
MANAGED BY	NORTHERN
PLATFORMS	2 (STAGGERED)
REQUEST STOP	NO
SERVICE FREQUENCY	MON-FRI SAT SUN B B X

STATION USAGE	NUMBER OF PASSENGERS	LEAST USED
2008/09	3946	166
2009/10	3954	164
2010/11	3684	153
2011/12	3512	142
2012/13	3982	155
2013/14	3146	129

Bescar Lane station is situated on the Manchester to Southport line four and a half miles from Southport. It serves the village of Scarisbrick located one mile away.

Northern provide all the services on the line. 142030 arrives with the 9.55 Southport-Stalybridge on 24 September 2013.

The station is well cared for with many flowers and plants on display. On 24 September 2013 142058/150270 depart with the 8.46 Manchester Victoria-Southport.

STYAL

OPENED	1 MAY 1909
PRE GROUPING	LONDON & NORTH WESTERN
MANAGED BY	NORTHERN
PLATFORMS	2
REQUEST STOP	NO
SERVICE	MON-FRI SAT SUN
FREQUENCY	C C B

STATION USAGE	NUMBER OF PASSENGERS	LEAST USED
2008/09	1228	80
2009/10	2206	119
2010/11	2440	125
2011/12	2790	126
2012/13	3660	148
2013/14	4226	153

Styal station is on the line between Wilmslow and Manchester Airport nine miles south of Manchester Piccadilly. Before the opening of the Manchester Airport Link, Styal had a service every half hour. It now receives just a peak hour service.

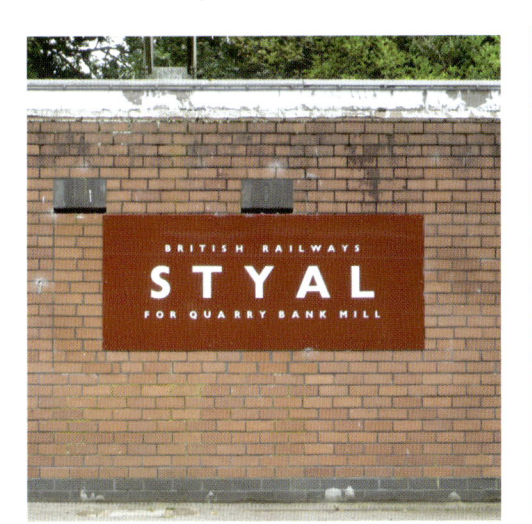

The line is electrified and is served by Northern Class 323 units. 323236 is ready to depart with the 7.53 Alderley Edge-Manchester Piccadilly on 20 September 2013.

On the same date 323225 calls with the 7.46 Manchester Piccadilly-Crewe.

Britains Least Used Stations 91

DOVE HOLES

OPENED	15 JUNE 1863
PRE GROUPING	LONDON & NORTH WESTERN
MANAGED BY	NORTHERN
PLATFORMS	2
REQUEST STOP	NO
SERVICE	MON-FRI SAT SUN
FREQUENCY	B B B

STATION USAGE	NUMBER OF PASSENGERS	LEAST USED
2008/09	5866	211
2009/10	5246	188
2010/11	5446	194
2011/12	6246	195
2012/13	5874	193
2013/14	4382	=154

Dove Holes station is on the Manchester Piccadilly to Buxton line. It is situated in the Peak District three miles north of Buxton. The station serves the village of Dove Holes which has a population of around 1200.

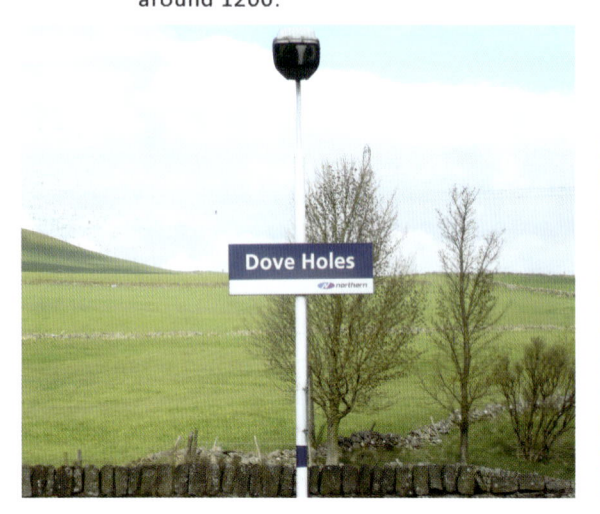

Northern Rail provide a two hourly service using class 150 or 156 DMUs. 150137/111 enter the station with the 8.52 Manchester Piccadilly - Buxton on 24 April 2012.

On the same date 156486 is about to leave with the 9.27 Buxton-Manchester Piccadilly.

Britains Least Used Stations

ASHLEY

OPENED	12 MAY 1862
PRE GROUPING	CHESHIRE LINES COMMITTE
MANAGED BY	NORTHERN
PLATFORMS	2
REQUEST STOP	NO
SERVICE	MON-FRI SAT SUN
FREQUENCY	A A B

STATION USAGE	NUMBER OF PASSENGERS	LEAST USED
2008/09	4740	185
2009/10	4328	173
2010/11	5478	195
2011/12	6676	200
2012/13	7174	208
2013/14	5856	188

Ashley station is situated on the Manchester Piccadilly to Chester line two and a half miles south of Altrincham. The station serves the village of Ashley which has a population of around 300. The station building has been converted into residential use.

For a small village Ashley enjoys an excellent service of one train every hour provided by Northern. 142038 arrives at the station with the 15.17 Manchester Piccadilly-Chester on 7 November 2013.

On the same date 150142 is ready to leave with the 14.53 Chester-Manchester Piccadilly.

Britains Least Used Stations

MOSS SIDE

OPENED	16 FEBRUARY 1846
PRE GROUPING	PRESTON & WYRE
MANAGED BY	NORTHERN
PLATFORMS	1
REQUEST STOP	NO
SERVICE	MON-FRI SAT SUN
FREQUENCY	A A A
	(X SUNDAY WINTER)
STATION USAGE	NUMBER OF PASSENGERS / LEAST USED
2008/09	3140 147
2009/10	3096 145
2010/11	3138 140
2011/12	2494 116
2012/13	2458 117
2013/14	2328 107

Moss Side station is situated on the Preston to Blackpool line between Lytham and Kirkham and Wesham. It serves the hamlet of Moss Side. In 1961 the station was closed along with Wrea Green. The platform at Moss Side was retained and in 1983 a grant from the Lancashire County Council enabled the station to be reopened.

Despite the low number of passengers the station receives a service every hour provided by Northern Rail. 150135/222 are ready to depart with the 10.23 Colne-Blackpool South on 6 June 2015.

The same units are seen returning with the 12.21 Blackpool South-Colne.

SALWICK

OPENED	16 JULY 1840
PRE GROUPING	PRESTON & WYRE
MANAGED BY	NORTHERN
PLATFORMS	2
REQUEST STOP	NO
SERVICE	MON-FRI SAT SUN
FREQUENCY	C C X

STATION USAGE	NUMBER OF PASSENGERS	LEAST USED
2008/09	2650	133
2009/10	1776	96
2010/11	1944	99
2011/12	2062	104
2012/13	2222	106
2013/14	2994	123

Salwick station is situated on the Preston to Blackpool line five miles west of Preston. The nearest village is over a mile away and the station is mainly used by workers at the nearby Springfield British Nuclear Fuel Complex.

Only a limited number of peak hour services call at Salwick. On 2 October 2008 142051 is seen departing with the 15.00 Colne-Blackpool South while 142054 arrives with the 15.53 Blackpool South-Colne.

Five years later on 24 October 2013 142053 arrives with the 15.44 Blackpool South-Colne.

Britains Least Used Stations 95

BRAYSTONES

OPENED	21 JULY 1849
PRE GROUPING	FURNESS
MANAGED BY	NORTHERN
PLATFORMS	1
REQUEST STOP	YES
SERVICE	MON-FRI SAT SUN
FREQUENCY	C C X

STATION USAGE	NUMBER OF PASSENGERS	LEAST USED
2008/09	1096	68
2009/10	1964	105
2010/11	1970	101
2011/12	966	54
2012/13	1046	58
2013/14	620	38

Braystones station is on the Cambrian Coast Line between Barrow in Furness and Carlisle nine miles south of Whitehaven. The station is situated on the coast in a remote location with very few houses nearby. The station building is now in private ownership.

Northern Rail provide all the services on the line. 142060 enters the station with the 12.41 Carlisle-Lancaster (via Barrow) on 9 October 2008.

On the same date 156438 heads north with the 10.10 Preston-Carlisle (via Barrow).

Britains Least Used Stations

NETHERTOWN

OPENED	21 JULY 1849
PRE GROUPING	FURNESS
MANAGED BY	NORTHERN
PLATFORMS	1
REQUEST STOP	YES
SERVICE	MON-FRI SAT SUN
FREQUENCY	C C X

STATION USAGE	NUMBER OF PASSENGERS	LEAST USED
2008/09	1020	63
2009/10	536	43
2010/11	450	36
2011/12	428	35
2012/13	1028	57
2013/14	1160	56

Nethertown station is on the Cumbrian Coast Line between Barrow in Furness and Carlisle. It is situated one and a half miles north of Braystones in an equally remote location on a small cliff overlooking the sea.

Nethertown has a limited service of four or five trains in each direction. 156448 approaches the station with the 14.20 Carlisle-Barrow on 15 October 2013.

On 9 October 2008 153317 is seen leaving Nethertown with the 10.14 Carlisle-Barrow.

Britains Least Used Stations 97

PARTON

OPENED	19 MARCH 1847
PRE GROUPING	LONDON & NORTH WESTERN
MANAGED BY	NORTHERN
PLATFORMS	2
REQUEST STOP	YES
SERVICE	MON-FRI SAT SUN
FREQUENCY	A A C

STATION USAGE	NUMBER OF PASSENGERS	LEAST USED
2008/09	4758	186
2009/10	8022	237
2010/11	6382	206
2011/12	6736	201
2012/13	6366	195
2013/14	5948	190

Parton station is on the Cumbrian Coast Line one and a half miles north of Whitehaven. The station serves the village of Parton which is situated on the coast overlooking the Irish Sea.

On 15 October 2013 156443 is seen arriving with the 9.10 Barrow-Carlisle.

Like most stations on the line Parton receives a service roughly every hour provided by Northern Rail. 153352 pauses with the 11.44 Carlisle-Whitehaven on 31 October 2008.

98   Britains Least Used Stations

HAWARDEN BRIDGE

OPENED	22 SEPTEMBER 1924
PRE GROUPING	LONDON & NORTH WESTERN
MANAGED BY	ARRIVA TRAINS WALES
PLATFORMS	2
REQUEST STOP	YES
SERVICE FREQUENCY	MON-FRI SAT SUN C C B

STATION USAGE	NUMBER OF PASSENGERS	LEAST USED
2008/09	9750	270
2009/10	6632	218
2010/11	4540	177
2011/12	4472	165
2012/13	5422	180
2013/14	4088	148

Hawarden Bridge station is on the line between Bidston and Wrexham Central. It is situated on the north side of Hawarden Bridge which crosses the River Dee.

The station is served by Arriva Trains Wales. Only morning and afternoon peak hour services call at the station with an improved service on Sunday. 150262 calls with the 16.35 Bidston-Wrexham Central on 4 March 2015.

On 26 August 2008 150254 is seen arriving with the 16.33 Wrexham Central - Bidston.

Britains Least Used Stations

GLAN CONWY

OPENED	17 JUNE 1863
PRE GROUPING	LONDON & NORTH WESTERN
MANAGED BY	ARRIVA TRAINS WALES
PLATFORMS	1
REQUEST STOP	YES
SERVICE FREQUENCY	MON-FRI SAT SUN B B C (X SUNDAY WINTER)
STATION USAGE	NUMBER OF PASSENGERS LEAST USED
2008/09	2342 124
2009/10	2404 126
2010/11	2416 123
2011/12	3798 149
2012/13	3288 138
2013/14	4572 161

Glan Conwy station is on the Conwy Valley Line between Llandudno and Blaenau Ffestiniog. It is situated on the east bank of the River Conwy two miles south of Llandudno Junction. The station was closed in October 1964 and reopened in May 1980.

Arriva Trains Wales Class 150 DMUs provide services on the line. On 29 August 2014 150252 heads towards Llandudno with the 11.46 from Blaenau Ffestiniog.

On the same date 150252 approaches Glan Conwy with the 13.08 Llandudno-Blaenau Ffestiniog.

TAL-Y-CAFN

OPENED	17 JUNE 1863
PRE GROUPING	LONDON & NORTH WESTERN
MANAGED BY	ARRIVA TRAINS WALES
PLATFORMS	1
REQUEST STOP	YES (NORTHBOUND)
SERVICE FREQUENCY	MON-FRI SAT SUN B B C (X SUNDAY WINTER)
STATION USAGE	NUMBER OF PASSENGERS / LEAST USED
2008/09	1240 / 81
2009/10	1078 / 65
2010/11	988 / 58
2011/12	1356 / 71
2012/13	1666 / 82
2013/14	2400 / 111

Tal-y-Cafn station is situated on the Conwy Valley Line four and a half miles south of Llandudno Junction station. The station serves the villages of Tal-y-Cafn and Eglwysbach.

The station opened as Tal-y-Cafn and Eglwysbach and was renamed Tal-y-Cafn in 1974. The name board on the disused platform still refers to Eglwybach.(right)

Tal-y- Cafn is a request stop for northbound services only. This is due to the manually operated level crossing at the south of the station. On 17 April 2009 150213 approaches the station over the crossing with the 17.37 Blaenau Ffestiniog-Llandudno. (below)

150252 is seen entering Tal-y-Cafn on 29 August 2014 with the 16.20 Llandudno-Blaenau Ffestiniog. (below right)

Britains Least Used Stations

DOLGARROG

OPENED	18 DECEMBER 1916
PRE GROUPING	LONDON & NORTH WESTERN
MANAGED BY	ARRIVA TRAINS WALES
PLATFORMS	1
REQUEST STOP	YES
SERVICE FREQUENCY	MON-FRI SAT SUN B B C (X SUNDAY WINTER)
STATION USAGE	NUMBER OF LEAST PASSENGERS USED
2008/09	664	48
2009/10	382	=32
2010/11	472	37
2011/12	612	41
2012/13	508	36
2013/14	828	45

Dolgarrog station is on the Conwy Valley Line eight and a half miles south of Llandudno Junction. The village of Dolgarrog is located one mile from the station on the opposite side of the River Conwy. Dolgarrog is currently the fourth least used station in Wales.

There are five or six services in each direction on weekdays. During the summer there are three services on Sunday but none during the winter. 150213 leaves Dolgarrog with the 16.20 Llandudno-Blaenau Ffestiniog on 17 April 2009.

102   *Britains Least Used Stations*

NORTH LLANRWST

OPENED	17 JUNE 1863
PRE GROUPING	LONDON & NORTH WESTERN
MANAGED BY	ARRIVA TRAINS WALES
PLATFORMS	2
REQUEST STOP	YES
SERVICE FREQUENCY	MON-FRI SAT SUN B B C (X SUNDAY WINTER)

STATION USAGE	NUMBER OF PASSENGERS	LEAST USED
2008/09	1116	71
2009/10	1086	66
2010/11	1236	68
2011/12	1272	64
2012/13	1966	95
2013/14	2204	105

North Llanrwst station is on the Conwy Valley Line midway between Llandudno and Blaenau Ffestiniog and is situated half a mile north of Llanrwst station. The station was once called Llanrwst as the only station serving the town but became North Llanrwst after a new station opened in the centre of the town in 1989.

North Llanrwst is the only station on the line with a passing loop and two platforms. 150213 stands in the northbound platform with the 11.52 Blaenau Ffestiniog-Llandudno on 17 April 2009.

On 29 August 2014 150252 calls with the 16.20 Llandudno-Blaenau Ffestiniog.

Britains Least Used Stations 103

PONT-Y-PANT

OPENED	22 JULY 1879
PRE GROUPING	LONDON & NORTH WESTERN
MANAGED BY	ARRIVA TRAINS WALES
PLATFORMS	1
REQUEST STOP	YES
SERVICE FREQUENCY	MON-FRI SAT SUN B B C (X SUNDAY WINTER)
STATION USAGE	NUMBER OF PASSENGERS	LEAST USED
2008/09	2134	117
2009/10	1576	85
2010/11	1472	75
2011/12	1426	76
2012/13	1704	85
2013/14	1424	71

Pont-y-Pant station is on the Conwy Valley Line four miles south of Betws-y-Coed. The station serves a small community situated a short distance away across the River Conwy. The station house is well maintained and used as a private dwelling.

On 29 August 2014 150252 pauses with the 13.08 Llandudno-Blaenau Ffestiniog.

150213 passes the station house as it departs Pont-y-Pant with the 13.20 Llandudno-Blaenau Ffestiniog on 17 April 2009.

DOLWYDDELAN

OPENED	22 JULY 1879
PRE GROUPING	LONDON & NORTH WESTERN
MANAGED BY	ARRIVA TRAINS WALES
PLATFORMS	1
REQUEST STOP	YES
SERVICE FREQUENCY	MON-FRI SAT SUN B B C (X SUNDAY WINTER)
STATION USAGE	NUMBER OF PASSENGERS	LEAST USED
2008/09	4780	188
2009/10	4210	172
2010/11	4952	183
2011/12	5326	182
2012/13	5506	184
2013/14	4184	152

Dolwyddelan station is on the Conwy Valley Line seven miles from Blaenau Ffestiniog. The village of Dolwyddelan is situated a short distance away across the River Conwy.

150213 approaches the station with the 14.52 Blaenau Ffestiniog-Llandudno on 17 April 2009.

Britains Least Used Stations

105

ROMAN BRIDGE

OPENED	22 JULY 1879
PRE GROUPING	LONDON & NORTH WESTERN
MANAGED BY	ARRIVA TRAINS WALES
PLATFORMS	1
REQUEST STOP	YES
SERVICE FREQUENCY	MON-FRI SAT SUN B B C (X SUNDAY WINTER)
STATION USAGE	NUMBER OF PASSENGERS — LEAST USED
2008/09	388 — =30
2009/10	610 — 45
2010/11	636 — 44
2011/12	780 — 50
2012/13	842 — 51
2013/14	764 — 42

Roman Bridge station is situated on the Conwy Valley Line five miles from Blaenau Ffestiniog. There are no houses nearby and the station is mainly used by walkers. The station takes its name from the nearby bridge over the River Lledr. Roman Bridge is currently the second least used station in Wales.

The station building is is in private ownership.

150252 pulls into the station with the 11.46 Blaenau Ffestiniog-Llandudno on 29 August 2014.

Britains Least Used Stations

INCE & ELTON

OPENED	1 JULY 1863
PRE GROUPING	BIRKENHEAD JOINT
MANAGED BY	NORTHERN
PLATFORMS	2
REQUEST STOP	NO
SERVICE	MON-FRI SAT SUN
FREQUENCY	C C X

STATION USAGE	NUMBER OF PASSENGERS	LEAST USED
2008/09	544	40
2009/10	296	=25
2010/11	532	41
2011/12	386	=31
2012/13	460	=32
2013/14	944	51

Ince and Elton station is on the line between Ellesmere Port and Helsby. It is situated between the two villages.

Ince and Elton has a service of two morning and two afternoon trains in each direction provided by Northern Rail. 142036 calls with the 16.03 Helsby-Ellesmere Port on 1 May 2008.

On 24 September 2013 156466 arrives with the 15.48 Helsby-Ellesmere Port.

Britains Least Used Stations 107

STANLOW & THORNTON

OPENED	23 DECEMBER 1940
PRE GROUPING	N/A
MANAGED BY	NORTHERN
PLATFORMS	2
REQUEST STOP	NO
SERVICE	MON-FRI SAT SUN
FREQUENCY	C C X

STATION USAGE	NUMBER OF PASSENGERS	LEAST USED
2008/09	480	34
2009/10	490	40
2010/11	342	28
2011/12	468	37
2012/13	260	22
2013/14	314	=23

Stanlow and Thornton station is on the line between Ellesmere Port and Helsby. The station is situated within the Stanlow Refinery and most station users are workers at the site.

Stanlow and Thornton receives the same service as Ince and Elton. Taken from the footbridge 156466 is seen with the 15.17 Helsby-Ellesmere Port on 24 September 2013.

The last afternoon service continues beyond Helsby. 142036 arrives with the 16.17 Ellesmere Port-Liverpool. Lime Street on 1 May 2008.

108   Britains Least Used Stations

LITTLE KIMBLE

OPENED	1 JUNE 1872
PRE GROUPING	GREAT WESTERN
MANAGED BY	CHILTERN
PLATFORMS	1
REQUEST STOP	NO
SERVICE	MON-FRI SAT SUN
FREQUENCY	A A A

STATION USAGE	NUMBER OF PASSENGERS	LEAST USED
2008/09	8262	246
2009/10	8234	242
2010/11	9354	246
2011/12	9858	248
2012/13	6696	203
2013/14	5262	179

Little Kimble station is one of two stations on the seven and a half mile line between Princes Risborough and Aylesbury and is 39 miles from London Marylebone. It is the nearest station to Chequers the country house retreat of the Prime Minister. In 1998 when the G8 Summit was being held in Birmingham it received the Royal Train with the wives of the world leaders including Cherie Blair and Hillary Clinton.

There is an hourly service for most of the day between Aylesbury and Princes Risborough with some through services to London Marylebone. Chiltern Class 165 are provided for services on the line. 165020 arrives with the 12.31 Aylesbury-Princes Risborough on 12 July 2014.

Britains Least Used Stations

109

CLAVERDON

OPENED	10 OCTOBER 1860
PRE GROUPING	GREAT WESTERN
MANAGED BY	LONDON MIDLAND
PLATFORMS	1
REQUEST STOP	NO
SERVICE	MON-FRI SAT SUN
FREQUENCY	B B X

STATION USAGE	NUMBER OF PASSENGERS	LEAST USED
2008/09	2042	113
2009/10	2006	=109
2010/11	2294	116
2011/12	2570	119
2012/13	2300	110
2013/14	2654	116

Claverdon station is on the line between Stratford-upon-Avon and Leamington Spa. The village of Claverdon is situated half a mile from the station. In 1939 the station was resited west of the overbridge.

Although Claverdon station is managed by London Midland most of its services are provided by Chiltern. 165030 pauses with the 17.09 Marylebone-Stratford-upon- Avon on 12 July 2014.

Taken from the bridge at the east of the station 168110 is seen arriving on 12 July 2014 with the 17.35 Stratford-upon-Avon- Marylebone.

110   *Britains Least Used Stations*

BEARLEY

OPENED	10 OCTOBER 1860
PRE GROUPING	GREAT WESTERN
MANAGED BY	LONDON MIDLAND
PLATFORMS	1
REQUEST STOP	NO
SERVICE	MON-FRI SAT SUN
FREQUENCY	B B X
STATION	NUMBER OF LEAST
USAGE	PASSENGERS USED
2008/09	1716 102
2009/10	1212 70
2010/11	944 56
2011/12	960 53
2012/13	670 43
2013/14	1220 =58

Bearley station is situated on the line between Stratford-upon-Avon and Leamington Spa. The station serves the small village of Bearley.

Bearley receives the same service as Claverdon. 165036 enters the station with the 11.40 Stratford-upon-Avon-Marylebone on 10 July 2009.

Five years later on 12 July 2014 taken from the same spot 168110 arrives with the 17.35 Stratford-upon-Avon-Marylebone.

Britains Least Used Stations 111

THORNFORD

OPENED	23 MARCH 1936
PRE GROUPING	GREAT WESTERN
MANAGED BY	FIRST GREAT WESTERN
PLATFORMS	1
REQUEST STOP	YES
SERVICE	MON-FRI SAT SUN
FREQUENCY	B B C

STATION USAGE	NUMBER OF PASSENGERS	LEAST USED
2008/09	2486	128
2009/10	3256	147
2010/11	2838	136
2011/12	2832	128
2012/13	3042	134
2013/14	2708	117

Thornford station is on The Heart of Wessex Line between Bristol Temple Meads and Weymouth three miles south of Yeovil Penn Mill. The station serves the village of Thornford.

The station opened as Thornford Bridge Halt. The halt was omitted in 1969 and it became just Thornford in 1974.

Thornford receives a two hourly service provided by First Great Western. On 25 August 2011 150261 coupled with 153380 calls with the 11.10 Weymouth-Gloucester.

Britains Least Used Stations

YETMINSTER

OPENED	20 JANUARY 1857
PRE GROUPING	GREAT WESTERN
MANAGED BY	FIRST GREAT WESTERN
PLATFORMS	1
REQUEST STOP	YES
SERVICE	MON-FRI SAT SUN
FREQUENCY	B B C

STATION USAGE	NUMBER OF PASSENGERS	LEAST USED
2008/09	5836	209
2009/10	6350	=210
2010/11	7306	=221
2011/12	7404	211
2012/13	6552	199
2013/14	7188	207

Yetminster station is on the Bristol Temple Meads to Weymouth line four miles south of Yeovil Pen Mill. It serves the village of Yetminster situated east of the station.

A view looking south in the direction of Weymouth.

Yetminster receives the same service as Thornford. 150123 arrives with the 10.42 Gloucester-Weymouth on 25 August 2011.

Britains Least Used Stations 113

CHETNOLE

OPENED	11 SEPTEMBER 1933
PRE GROUPING	N/A
MANAGED BY	FIRST GREAT WESTERN
PLATFORMS	1
REQUEST STOP	YES
SERVICE	MON-FRI SAT SUN
FREQUENCY	B B C

STATION USAGE	NUMBER OF PASSENGERS	LEAST USED
2008/09	1944	111
2009/10	2132	117
2010/11	2386	121
2011/12	2206	108
2012/13	2358	115
2013/14	2398	110

Chetnole station is situated on the line between Bristol Temple Meads and Weymouth. The station is 21 miles north of Weymouth and serves the village of Chetnole and other local communities.

Most services originate or end at Gloucester. 153380/150261 pulls into Chetnole with the 11.10 Weymouth-Gloucester on 25 August 2011.

On the same date 150266/158766 are ready to leave with the 8.42 Gloucester-Weymouth

114   Britains Least Used Stations

COMBE

OPENED	8 JULY 1935
PRE GROUPING	N/A
MANAGED BY	FIRST GREAT WESTERN
PLATFORMS	1
REQUEST STOP	NO
SERVICE	MON-FRI SAT SUN
FREQUENCY	D X X

STATION USAGE	NUMBER OF PASSENGERS	LEAST USED
2008/09	2120	116
2009/10	1836	102
2010/11	2546	127
2011/12	2838	129
2012/13	2112	100
2013/14	1684	82

Combe station is situated on the line between Oxford and Worcester eight miles north west of Oxford. It is one of four stations on the Cotswold Line with a limited service. The station serves the village of Combe situated half a mile north of the station.

A First Great Western HST approaches the station with the 10.22 Paddington-Hereford on 16 July 2009.

Britains Least Used Stations

FINSTOCK

OPENED	9 APRIL 1934
PRE GROUPING	GREAT WESTERN
MANAGED BY	FIRST GREAT WESTERN
PLATFORMS	1
REQUEST STOP	NO
SERVICE	MON-FRI SAT SUN
FREQUENCY	D X X

STATION USAGE	NUMBER OF PASSENGERS	LEAST USED
2008/09	1022	64
2009/10	1458	78
2010/11	1984	102
2011/12	1982	98
2012/13	1970	96
2013/14	1920	92

Finstock station is on the line between Oxford and Worcester 12 miles north west of Oxford. The station is situated between the village of Finstock and the hamlet of Fawler.

The station was opened as Finstock Halt. The halt was removed in 1969 when it became just Finstock.

Finstock receives one morning service to Oxford and one evening service to Worcester. A First Great Western Class 165 speeds through Finstock with the 12.06 Worcester Foregate Street-Paddington on 16 July 2009.

Britains Least Used Stations

ASCOTT-UNDER-WYCHWOOD

OPENED	4 JUNE 1853
PRE GROUPING	GREAT WESTERN
MANAGED BY	FIRST GREAT WESTERN
PLATFORMS	2
REQUEST STOP	NO
SERVICE	MON-FRI SAT SUN
FREQUENCY	D X X

STATION USAGE	NUMBER OF PASSENGERS	LEAST USED
2008/09	2860	138
2009/10	2264	121
2010/11	1658	86
2011/12	2702	123
2012/13	2484	118
2013/14	2856	120

Ascott-under-Wychwood station is situated on the Oxford to Worcester line 17 miles north west of Oxford. The station serves the small village of Ascott-under-Wychwood. In 2011 the line was doubled and a second platform built.

The signal box controls the level crossing and the line beyond.

A First Great Western HST speeds past the narrow platform with the 13.11 Hereford-Paddington on 16 July 2009 prior to the building of the new platform.

Britains Least Used Stations

117

SHIPTON

OPENED	4 JUNE 1853
PRE GROUPING	GREAT WESTERN
MANAGED BY	FIRST GREAT WESTERN
PLATFORMS	2
REQUEST STOP	NO
SERVICE	MON-FRI SAT SUN
FREQUENCY	C C X

STATION USAGE	NUMBER OF PASSENGERS	LEAST USED
2008/09	3032	142
2009/10	2890	141
2010/11	3614	149
2011/12	4680	169
2012/13	5028	173
2013/14	5050	177

Shipton station is on the Oxford to Worcester line 18 miles from Oxford. It serves the village of Shipton-under Wychwood. The station is situated on the double track section of the line between Ascott-under- Wychwood and Evesham.

On 16 July 2009 166215 passes through Shipton with the 16.14 Moreton-in-March-Didcot Parkway.

Shipton receives a weekday service of two trains in each direction. HST 43190 pulls into the station with the 15.11 Hereford-Paddington on 16 July 2009.

Britains Least Used Stations

MAESTEG EWENNY ROAD

OPENED	26 OCTOBER 1992
PRE GROUPING	N/A
MANAGED BY	ARRIVA TRAINS WALES
PLATFORMS	1
REQUEST STOP	NO
SERVICE	MON-FRI SAT SUN
FREQUENCY	A A X

STATION USAGE	NUMBER OF PASSENGERS	LEAST USED
2008/09	4364	178
2009/10	4898	183
2010/11	3936	161
2011/12	4356	163
2012/13	2706	124
2013/14	3930	143

Maesteg Ewenny Road station is on the branch line between Bridgend and Maesteg. It is located half a mile from Maesteg station adjacent to the Ewenny Road Industrial Estate. The Maesteg Line was closed in 1970. When the line reopened in 1992 Maesteg Ewenny Road was one of four new stations to open on the line.

Arriva Trains Wales provide an hourly service. 150257 pauses with the 12.15 Maesteg - Cheltenham Spa on 4 May 2010.

With the destination board already changed in preparation for its next journey 150245 is heading for Maesteg with the 14.21 service from Cardiff on 26 August 2014.

Britains Least Used Stations

PENALLY

OPENED	OCTOBER 1863
PRE GROUPING	GREAT WESTERN
MANAGED BY	ARRIVA TRAINS WALES
PLATFORMS	1
REQUEST STOP	YES
SERVICE FREQUENCY	MON-FRI SAT SUN B B C

STATION USAGE	NUMBER OF PASSENGERS	LEAST USED
2008/09	5012	191
2009/10	5680	=199
2010/11	4676	179
2011/12	5486	184
2012/13	5136	176
2013/14	4506	159

Penally station is in south west Wales on the branch line between Whitland and Pembroke Dock. It is situated one mile from Tenby and serves the coastal village of Penally.

Penally station was closed in June 1964 but reopened in June 1970. It was also closed during the winters of 1971 and 1972.

Arriva Trains Wales provide a two hourly service. 153303/362 arrive at Penally with the 10.05 Swansea -Pembroke Dock on 3 June 2011.

Britains Least Used Stations

LAMPHEY

OPENED	6 AUGUST 1863
PRE GROUPING	GREAT WESTERN
MANAGED BY	ARRIVA TRAINS WALES
PLATFORMS	1
REQUEST STOP	YES
SERVICE	MON-FRI SAT SUN
FREQUENCY	B B C

STATION USAGE	NUMBER OF PASSENGERS	LEAST USED
2008/09	4320	176
2009/10	4446	176
2010/11	4342	175
2011/12	4482	166
2012/13	3812	150
2013/14	4986	173

Lamphey station is situated on the line between Whitland and Pembroke Dock three and a half miles from Pembroke Dock. It serves the village of Lamphey which has a population of around 300.

A view of the platform taken from the overbridge looking towards Pembroke.

Lamphey receives the same service as Penally. 142082 arrives with the 12.00 Swansea-Pembroke Dock on 2 June 2011.

Britains Least Used Stations 121

JOHNSTON

OPENED	15 APRIL 1856
PRE GROUPING	GREAT WESTERN
MANAGED BY	ARRIVA TRAINS WALES
PLATFORMS	1
REQUEST STOP	YES
SERVICE	MON-FRI SAT SUN
FREQUENCY	B B B

STATION USAGE	NUMBER OF PASSENGERS	LEAST USED
2008/09	5822	208
2009/10	6446	216
2010/11	6762	210
2011/12	6476	199
2012/13	7216	209
2013/14	8326	=222

Johnston station is situated on the West Wales Line four miles from the terminus at Milford Haven. In the past the station has had various names including Milford Road, Johnston (Pembroke) and Johnston (Dyfed).

Johnston is served by Arriva Trains Wales with a two hourly service between Manchester Piccadilly and Milford Haven. 175001 runs into the station on 3 June 2010 with the 13.08 Milford Haven-Manchester Piccadilly.

175001 is now ready to depart on its six hour journey to Manchester.

Britains Least Used Stations

BROOME

OPENED	6 MARCH 1861
PRE GROUPING	LONDON & NORTH WESTERN
MANAGED BY	ARRIVA TRAINS WALES
PLATFORMS	1
REQUEST STOP	YES
SERVICE FREQUENCY	MON-FRI SAT SUN C C C

STATION USAGE	NUMBER OF PASSENGERS	LEAST USED
2008/09	1830	105
2009/10	1622	88
2010/11	1642	85
2011/12	1472	79
2012/13	1620	79
2013/14	1990	96

Broome is the first station after Craven Arms on the Heart of Wales Line. Situated 23 miles from Shrewsbury it is one of four stations on the line in England. The station serves the villages of Broome and Aston on Clun.

Classes 150 or 153 DMUs are provided for services on the line. 153327 pauses with the 13.16 Swansea-Shrewsbury on 26 May 2011.

Later the same day 153327 is seen returning to Swansea with the 18.05 from Shrewsbury.

Britains Least Used Stations

HOPTON HEATH

OPENED	6 MARCH 1861
PRE GROUPING	LONDON & NORTH WESTERN
MANAGED BY	ARRIVA TRAINS WALES
PLATFORMS	1
REQUEST STOP	YES
SERVICE	MON-FRI SAT SUN
FREQUENCY	C C C

STATION USAGE	NUMBER OF PASSENGERS	LEAST USED
2008/09	1268	84
2009/10	680	=51
2010/11	1074	63
2011/12	1554	=81
2012/13	2244	108
2013/14	2990	122

Hopton Heath station is on the Heart of Wales Line 25 miles from Shrewsbury. The station serves a number of small villages including Clungunford, Beckjay and Hopton Heath. The station buildings are in private ownership

Some services originate or terminate at Cardiff. On 26 May 2011 150281 leaves Hopton Heath with the 8.09 Cardiff -Shrewsbury.

Britains Least Used Stations

BUCKNELL

OPENED	6 MARCH 1861
PRE GROUPING	LONDON & NORTH WESTERN
MANAGED BY	ARRIVA TRAINS WALES
PLATFORMS	1
REQUEST STOP	YES
SERVICE FREQUENCY	MON-FRI SAT SUN C C C

STATION USAGE	NUMBER OF PASSENGERS	LEAST USED
2008/09	3482	152
2009/10	3798	158
2010/11	4228	168
2011/12	4486	167
2012/13	5478	183
2013/14	5806	187

Bucknell station is on the Heart of Wales Line 28 miles south west of Shrewsbury and four miles from the Welsh border at Knighton. The village of Bucknell is located to the north of the station. The station building is in private ownership.

150281 is seen arriving at Bucknell with the 14.04 Shrewsbury-Swansea on 26 May 2011.

Britains Least Used Stations

KNUCKLAS

OPENED	1 DECEMBER 1865
PRE GROUPING	LONDON & NORTH WESTERN
MANAGED BY	ARRIVA TRAINS WALES
PLATFORMS	1
REQUEST STOP	YES
SERVICE	MON-FRI SAT SUN
FREQUENCY	C C C

STATION USAGE	NUMBER OF PASSENGERS	LEAST USED
2008/09	4572	181
2009/10	3644	151
2010/11	3998	=163
2011/12	4994	172
2012/13	4504	166
2013/14	4778	=168

Knucklas is the first station in Wales on the Heart of Wales Line two and a half miles west of Knighton. Departing Knucklas in a westerly direction the line crosses the Knucklas Viaduct.

150281 pauses with the 8.09 Cardiff-Shrewsbury on 26 May 2011.

In fading light 153367 calls with the 18.05 Shrewsbury-Swansea on 27 August 2014.

LLANGYNLLO

OPENED	MARCH 1866
PRE GROUPING	LONDON & NORTH WESTERN
MANAGED BY	ARRIVA TRAINS WALES
PLATFORMS	1
REQUEST STOP	YES
SERVICE	MON-FRI SAT SUN
FREQUENCY	C C C

STATION USAGE	NUMBER OF PASSENGERS	LEAST USED
2008/09	918	58
2009/10	966	59
2010/11	1032	=59
2011/12	1046	57
2012/13	958	54
2013/14	806	44

Llangynllo station (sometimes spelt Llangunllo) is on the Heart of Wales Line six and a half miles west of Knighton. The village of Llangunllo is located one mile south of the station. The highest point on the line at 980 feet above sea level is to be found north of the station.

153312 pauses with the 8.09 Cardiff-Shrewsbury on 1 June 2011.

Britains Least Used Stations

LLANBISTER ROAD

OPENED	JUNE 1868
PRE GROUPING	LONDON & NORTH WESTERN
MANAGED BY	ARRIVA TRAINS WALES
PLATFORMS	1
REQUEST STOP	YES
SERVICE FREQUENCY	MON-FRI SAT SUN C C C

STATION USAGE	NUMBER OF PASSENGERS	LEAST USED
2008/09	1566	98
2009/10	1668	91
2010/11	1172	66
2011/12	1554	=81
2012/13	1596	76
2013/14	1390	68

Llanbister Road station is on the Heart of Wales Line midway between Knucklas and Llandrindod Wells. The village of Llanbister is located five miles east of the station.

150281 calls with the 14.04 Shrewsbury-Swansea on 26 May 2011.

DOLAU

OPENED	1 DECEMBER 1865
PRE GROUPING	LONDON & NORTH WESTERN
MANAGED BY	ARRIVA TRAINS WALES
PLATFORMS	1
REQUEST STOP	YES
SERVICE	MON-FRI SAT SUN
FREQUENCY	C C C

STATION USAGE	NUMBER OF PASSENGERS	LEAST USED
2008/09	1146	75
2009/10	2064	113
2010/11	2430	124
2011/12	1658	85
2012/13	1520	73
2013/14	1406	69

Dolau station is on the Heart of Wales Line six and a half miles north east of Llandrindod Wells. The station serves the small village of Dolau located south of the station.

Dolau station is beautifully cared for by a group of enthusiastic volunteers known as the Dolau Station Action Group. The station has won numerous awards for its floral displays including best kept unmanned station in the UK.

A small wooden hut displays all the awards and has a guest book for visitors to sign. (below)

The Queen unveiled a plaque at the station in 2002 commemorating her visit during her Golden Jubilee trip to Wales. (below right)

Britains Least Used Stations

DOLAU

150281 pauses with the 14.04 Shrewsbury-Swansea on 26 May 2011. (right)

On the same date 153327 arrives with the 13.16 Swansea-Shrewsbury. (below)

PEN-Y-BONT

OPENED	1 DECEMBER 1865
PRE GROUPING	LONDON & NORTH WESTERN
MANAGED BY	ARRIVA TRAINS WALES
PLATFORMS	1
REQUEST STOP	YES
SERVICE	MON-FRI SAT SUN
FREQUENCY	C C C

STATION USAGE	NUMBER OF PASSENGERS	LEAST USED
2008/09	1462	89
2009/10	1542	82
2010/11	1490	78
2011/12	1652	84
2012/13	1444	68
2013/14	1548	75

Pen-y-Bont station is on the Heart of Wales Line three miles north west of Llandrindod Wells. The village of Pen-y-Bont is located over a mile from the station.

153312 runs into the station with the 8.09 Cardiff-Shrewsbury on 1 June 2011.

On the same date 150284 calls with the 9.00 Shrewsbury-Cardiff.

Britains Least Used Stations   131

CILMERI

OPENED	11 MARCH 1867
PRE GROUPING	LONDON & NORTH WESTERN
MANAGED BY	ARRIVA TRAINS WALES
PLATFORMS	1
REQUEST STOP	YES
SERVICE	MON-FRI SAT SUN
FREQUENCY	C C C

STATION USAGE	NUMBER OF PASSENGERS	LEAST USED
2008/09	1530	=93
2009/10	1690	92
2010/11	1690	89
2011/12	1830	93
2012/13	1776	88
2013/14	1998	97

Cilmeri station is on the Heart of Wales Line eight miles south west of Llandrindod Wells. The station serves the small village of Cilmeri and is three miles from Builth Wells. Until 1980 the station was spelt as Cilmery.

On 27 August 2014 153367 pauses with the 5.16 Shrewsbury-Swansea.

In fading light 150281 is ready to leave with the 18.21 Swansea-Shrewsbury on 26 May 2011.

132   Britains Least Used Stations

GARTH (POWYS)

OPENED	11 MARCH 1867
PRE GROUPING	LONDON & NORTH WESTERN
MANAGED BY	ARRIVA TRAINS WALES
PLATFORMS	1
REQUEST STOP	YES
SERVICE	MON-FRI SAT SUN
FREQUENCY	C C C

STATION USAGE	NUMBER OF PASSENGERS	LEAST USED
2008/09	1246	82
2009/10	1064	=63
2010/11	1032	=59
2011/12	1278	65
2012/13	1256	65
2013/14	1322	63

Garth (Powys) station is on the Heart of Wales Line eleven miles south west of Llandrindod Wells. The station serves the small village of Garth. The station is known as Garth (Powys) to differentiate it from Garth (Mid Glamorgan) on the Maesteg Line.

153327 calls with the 18.05 Shrewsbury- Swansea on 26 May 2011.

On the same date 150281 arrives at Garth with the 18.21 Swansea- Shrewsbury.

Britains Least Used Stations

LLANGAMMARCH

OPENED	SEPTEMBER 1867
PRE GROUPING	LONDON & NORTH WESTERN
MANAGED BY	ARRIVA TRAINS WALES
PLATFORMS	1
REQUEST STOP	YES
SERVICE	MON-FRI SAT SUN
FREQUENCY	C C C

STATION USAGE	NUMBER OF PASSENGERS	LEAST USED
2008/09	3270	151
2009/10	2324	124
2010/11	3146	142
2011/12	2998	132
2012/13	2674	123
2013/14	3126	128

Llangammarch station is on the Heart of Wales Line 13 miles south west of Llandrindod Wells. The station used to be called Llangammarch Wells after the village it serves. The station sign is still shown as Llangammarch Wells.

153303 is ready to leave with the 9.00 Shrewsbury- Cardiff on 26 May 2011.

Britains Least Used Stations

SUGAR LOAF

OPENED	10 JUNE 1909
PRE GROUPING	LONDON & NORTH WESTERN
MANAGED BY	ARRIVA TRAINS WALES
PLATFORMS	1
REQUEST STOP	YES
SERVICE	MON-FRI SAT SUN
FREQUENCY	C C C

STATION USAGE	NUMBER OF PASSENGERS	LEAST USED
2008/09	120	8
2009/10	106	5
2010/11	84	=9
2011/12	120	10
2012/13	144	12
2013/14	240	19

Sugar Loaf station is on the Heart of Wales Line 19 miles south west of Llandrindod Wells. It is the remotest station on the Heart of Wales Line and the least used station in Wales. The station is situated one mile from a small hill known as Sugar Loaf a popular viewpoint and picnic spot.

153327 is seen leaving with the 8.09 Cardiff-Shrewsbury on 27 May 2011.

On the same date 153320 arrives with the 9.00 Shrewsbury-Swansea.

Britains Least Used Stations 135

CYNGHORDY

OPENED	8 JUNE 1868
PRE GROUPING	LONDON & NORTH WESTERN
MANAGED BY	ARRIVA TRAINS WALES
PLATFORMS	1
REQUEST STOP	YES
SERVICE FREQUENCY	MON-FRI SAT SUN C C C

STATION USAGE	NUMBER OF PASSENGERS	LEAST USED
2008/09	1660	100
2009/10	1396	76
2010/11	1628	83
2011/12	1166	60
2012/13	1752	87
2013/14	1312	62

Cynghordy station is on the Heart of Wales Line 23 miles south west of Llandrindod Wells. The station serves a small community.

150285 is ready to leave with the 13.16 Swansea-Shrewsbury on 27 May 2011. It will soon cross the Cynghordy Viaduct which affords splendid views of the surrounding countryside.

Heading south on the same day 153327 pauses with the 14.04 Shrewsbury-Swansea.

Britains Least Used Stations

LLANWRDA

OPENED	1 APRIL 1858
PRE GROUPING	VALE OF TOWY JOINT
MANAGED BY	ARRIVA TRAINS WALES
PLATFORMS	1
REQUEST STOP	YES (SOUTHBOUND)
SERVICE	MON-FRI SAT SUN
FREQUENCY	C C C

STATION USAGE	NUMBER OF PASSENGERS	LEAST USED
2008/09	2214	120
2009/10	2358	125
2010/11	2268	114
2011/12	2082	105
2012/13	2210	104
2013/14	2066	99

Llanwrda station is on the Heart of Wales Line 27 miles north west of Llanelly. The station opened as Lampeter Road but was renamed Llanwrda in 1868 after the village it serves.

153353 calls with the 9.14 Swansea -Shrewsbury on 27 August 2014.

On the same date 150254 is seen arriving at Llanwrda with the 9.00 Shrewsbury-Cardiff.

Britains Least Used Stations

LLANGADOG

OPENED	1 APRIL 1858
PRE GROUPING	VALE OF TOWY JOINT
MANAGED BY	ARRIVA TRAINS WALES
PLATFORMS	1
REQUEST STOP	YES (SOUTHBOUND)
SERVICE	MON-FRI SAT SUN
FREQUENCY	C C C

STATION USAGE	NUMBER OF PASSENGERS	LEAST USED
2008/09	5736	206
2009/10	5464	192
2010/11	5436	193
2011/12	5512	185
2012/13	5558	186
2013/14	6094	191

Llangadog station is on the Heart of Wales Line 25 miles north west of Llanelli. The station serves the village of Llangadog situated to the east of the station.

150254 is ready to leave with the 9.00 Shrewsbury-Cardiff on 27 August 2014.

On the same date 153367 is seen at Llangadog with the 13.15 Swansea- Shrewsbury.

Britains Least Used Stations

FFAIRFACH

OPENED	26 JANUARY 1857
PRE GROUPING	GREAT WESTERN
MANAGED BY	ARRIVA TRAINS WALES
PLATFORMS	1
REQUEST STOP	YES
SERVICE	MON-FRI SAT SUN
FREQUENCY	C C C
STATION USAGE	NUMBER OF PASSENGERS / LEAST USED
2008/09	2198 / 118
2009/10	2616 / 133
2010/11	2302 / 117
2011/12	2490 / 115
2012/13	2568 / 121
2013/14	3146 / =129

Ffairfach station is on the Heart of Wales Line 19 miles north west of Llanelli and one mile south of the small town of Llandillo. The station serves the village of Ffairfach.

Two views of 150285 with the 13.16 Swansea-Shrewsbury on 27 May 2011. First seen entering Ffairfach over the level crossing (right) and second waiting in the platform ready to leave. (below)

Britains Least Used Stations 139

PANTYFFYNNON

OPENED	26 JANUARY 1857
PRE GROUPING	GREAT WESTERN
MANAGED BY	ARRIVA TRAINS WALES
PLATFORMS	1
REQUEST STOP	NO
SERVICE	MON-FRI SAT SUN
FREQUENCY	C C C

STATION USAGE	NUMBER OF PASSENGERS	LEAST USED
2008/09	3672	155
2009/10	3872	161
2010/11	4270	170
2011/12	3886	150
2012/13	4388	162
2013/14	4778	=168

Pantyffynnon station is on the Heart of Wales Line 12 miles north west of Llanelli and one mile south of Ammanford. The station serves the village of Pantyffynnon. The station once had three platforms and was the junction for the Amman Valley Branch but this closed to passengers in 1958.

The Amman Valley Line is seen branching off to the right. Now only occasional freight services use the line.

The station was being refurbished when 153367 was seen leaving with the 5.16 Shrewsbury-Swansea service on 27 August 2014.

140 — Britains Least Used Stations

PONTARDDULAIS

OPENED	1 MAY 1850
PRE GROUPING	GREAT WESTERN
MANAGED BY	ARRIVA TRAINS WALES
PLATFORMS	1
REQUEST STOP	YES
SERVICE	MON-FRI SAT SUN
FREQUENCY	C C C

STATION USAGE	NUMBER OF PASSENGERS	LEAST USED
2008/09	4122	169
2009/10	4414	175
2010/11	5052	185
2011/12	4272	160
2012/13	4404	163
2013/14	4692	166

Pontarddulais station is on the Heart of Wales Line seven miles from Llanelli. The station serves the town of Pontarddulais and the village of Hendy. Pontarddulais was once the junction for a line to Swansea Victoria but this fell victim of the Beeching axe in 1964.

153327 arrives with the 18.21 Swansea-Shrewsbury on 27 May 2011.

Britains Least Used Stations

LLANGENNECH

OPENED	1 MAY 1850
PRE GROUPING	GREAT WESTERN
MANAGED BY	ARRIVA TRAINS WALES
PLATFORMS	2
REQUEST STOP	YES
SERVICE	MON-FRI SAT SUN
FREQUENCY	C C C

STATION USAGE	NUMBER OF PASSENGERS	LEAST USED
2008/09	1362	87
2009/10	1596	87
2010/11	1834	93
2011/12	2004	100
2012/13	2006	97
2013/14	2908	121

Llangennech station is on the Heart of Wales Line just under five miles from Llanelli. It serves the village of Llangennech situated half a mile from the station. Llangennech and Bynea are the only stations to be on the double track section of the line.

On 27 May 2011 153327 pauses at Llangennech with the 14.04 Shrewsbury-Swansea.

BYNEA

OPENED	1 MAY 1850
PRE GROUPING	GREAT WESTERN
MANAGED BY	ARRIVA TRAINS WALES
PLATFORMS	2
REQUEST STOP	YES
SERVICE	MON-FRI SAT SUN
FREQUENCY	C C C

STATION USAGE	NUMBER OF PASSENGERS	LEAST USED
2008/09	1300	85
2009/10	1664	90
2010/11	1376	71
2011/12	1430	77
2012/13	1490	72
2013/14	1662	=80

Bynea is the final station on the Heart of Wales Line just under three miles from Llanelli. The station serves the village of Bynea.

Taken from the bridge at the south of the station 150285 is seen with the 5.19 Shrewsbury-Swansea on 27 May 2011.

On the same date 153327 runs into Bynea with the 8.09 Cardiff-Shrewsbury.

Britains Least Used Stations

GILFACH FARGOED

OPENED	APRIL 1908
PRE GROUPING	RHYMNEY
MANAGED BY	ARRIVA TRAINS WALES
PLATFORMS	2
REQUEST STOP	NO
SERVICE	MON-FRI SAT SUN
FREQUENCY	A A B

STATION USAGE	NUMBER OF PASSENGERS	LEAST USED
2008/09	2344	125
2009/10	3396	148
2010/11	3376	146
2011/12	4182	157
2012/13	3456	143
2013/14	3690	137

Gilfach Fargoed station is situated on the Rhymney Line in the Welsh Valleys 16 miles north of Cardiff. The station serves the village of Gilfach. At around 20 yards in length Gilfach Fargoed has one of the shortest platforms on the network.

Services are provided by Arriva Trains Wales using Class 142, 144 or 150 DMUs. On 26 August 2014 150250 is waiting to leave with the 10.47 Penarth-Bargoed.

142081 approaches Gilfach Fargoed on 8 April 2010 with the 16.17 Bargoed-Penarth.

Britains Least Used Stations

PREES

OPENED	SEPTEMBER 1858
PRE GROUPING	LONDON & NORTH WESTERN
MANAGED BY	ARRIVA TRAINS WALES
PLATFORMS	2
REQUEST STOP	YES
SERVICE FREQUENCY	MON-FRI SAT SUN B B C

STATION USAGE	NUMBER OF PASSENGERS	LEAST USED
2008/09	8112	242
2009/10	8362	243
2010/11	8614	236
2011/12	8668	230
2012/13	5112	175
2013/14	4892	=170

Prees station is on the Welsh Marshes Line between Crewe and Shrewsbury. The village of Prees is situated one mile from the station.

Arriva Trains Wales operate services on the line with Prees receiving a two hourly service. 153353 arrives in the station with the 11.20 Crewe-Shrewsbury on 26 March 2014. Note the steps to enable passengers to board and alight from the low platform. (below)

Manchester to South Wales services pass through Prees. 175114 hurries through the station with the 6.00 Milford Haven-Manchester Piccadilly on 26 March 2014. (below right)

Britains Least Used Stations   145

PILNING

OPENED	1 DECEMBER 1886
PRE GROUPING	GREAT WESTERN
MANAGED BY	FIRST GREAT WESTERN
PLATFORMS	2
REQUEST STOP	NO
SERVICE FREQUENCY	MON-FRI SAT SUN X E X

STATION USAGE	NUMBER OF PASSENGERS	LEAST USED
2008/09	130	9
2009/10	166	=10
2010/11	178	18
2011/12	146	13
2012/13	130	11
2013/14	88	8

Pilning station is on the line between Bristol Temple Meads and Cardiff two miles east of the Severn Tunnel. The village of Pilning is around one mile away and most of the village is situated nearer to Severn Beach station on the Severn Beach Line to Bristol. The station was known as Pilning High Level between 1928 and 1968.

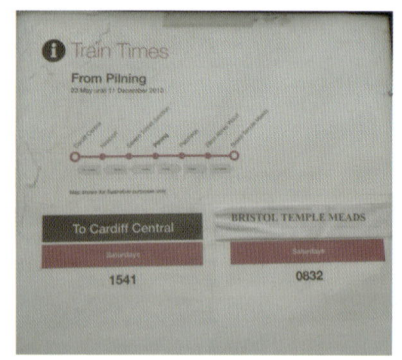

Pilning receives a parliamentary service of one train per week in each direction on Saturday.

First Great Western Class 150 DMU no 150125 calls with the 15.21 Bristol Temple Meads-Cardiff on 24 July 2010.

Paddington-South Wales services pass through Pilning. A First Great Western HST is seen speeding through the station on 24 July 2010 with the 13.28 Swansea Paddington.

ST BUDEAUX FERRY ROAD

OPENED	1 JUNE 1904
PRE GROUPING	GREAT WESTERN
MANAGED BY	FIRST GREAT WESTERN
PLATFORMS	2
REQUEST STOP	NO
SERVICE	MON-FRI SAT SUN
FREQUENCY	C C D

STATION USAGE	NUMBER OF PASSENGERS	LEAST USED
2008/09	1132	72
2009/10	1540	81
2010/11	2326	118
2011/12	3552	144
2012/13	3822	151
2013/14	4754	167

St Budeaux Ferry Road station is on the Cornish Main Line three miles west of Plymouth and one mile from where the line crosses the Royal Albert Bridge into Cornwall. St. Budeaux Victoria Road station on the Gunnislake branch is situated a few yards away and has a more frequent service to Plymouth.

First Great Western provide a limited service of four trains in each direction. 150106/153327 pull away from the station with the 9.30 Exeter Central-Penzance on 17 July 2014.

Most local services on the Cornish Main Line are in the hands of Class 150 DMUs. 150213 runs into St. Budeaux Ferry Road with the 17.06 Plymouth- Liskeard on 9 May 2008.

Britains Least Used Stations

MENHENIOT

OPENED	4 MAY 1859
PRE GROUPING	GREAT WESTERN
MANAGED BY	FIRST GREAT WESTERN
PLATFORMS	2
REQUEST STOP	YES
SERVICE	MON-FRI SAT SUN
FREQUENCY	C C D

STATION USAGE	NUMBER OF PASSENGERS	LEAST USED
2008/09	4598	182
2009/10	3844	160
2010/11	2690	132
2011/12	2398	114
2012/13	2324	113
2013/14	4064	146

Menheniot station is situated on the Cornish Main Line fourteen miles west of Plymouth. The station serves the village of Menheniot located half a mile north of the station.

First Great Western provide a limited service. All westbound services are in the afternoon. 153333/150244 depart with the 15.57 Plymouth-Penzance on 18 June 2013.

One hour later 150122 arrives at Menheniot with the 17.04 Plymouth-Liskeard.

NEWTON ST. CYRES

OPENED	OCTOBER 1851
PRE GROUPING	LONDON & SOUTH WESTERN
MANAGED BY	FIRST GREAT WESTERN
PLATFORMS	1
REQUEST STOP	YES
SERVICE FREQUENCY	MON-FRI SAT SUN C C C

STATION USAGE	NUMBER OF PASSENGERS	LEAST USED
2008/09	1868	108
2009/10	1784	97
2010/11	2774	135
2011/12	3212	136
2012/13	2252	109
2013/14	2760	119

Newton St Cyres is the first of eleven intermediate stations on the Tarka Line between Exeter St Davids and Barnstaple. It is located four and a half miles north of Exeter St Davids and serves the village of Newton St Cyres situated half a mile away. The station opened as St Cyres the Newton being added in 1913.

All the stations on the Tarka Line are beautifully kept with plenty of flowers on view.

Most of the services to call at the station are in the evening. In fading light 142029 pauses with the 20.55 Exeter Central-Barnstaple on 16 June 2009.(below)

On 11 June 2015 143619 hurries through the station with the 11.53 Exmouth-Barnstaple.(below right)

Britains Least Used Stations   149

LAPFORD

OPENED	1 AUGUST 1854
PRE GROUPING	LONDON & SOUTH WESTERN
MANAGED BY	FIRST GREAT WESTERN
PLATFORMS	1
REQUEST STOP	YES
SERVICE FREQUENCY	MON-FRI SAT SUN C C C

STATION USAGE	NUMBER OF PASSENGERS	LEAST USED
2008/09	2058	114
2009/10	1878	104
2010/11	2374	119
2011/12	2062	=103
2012/13	1796	89
2013/14	2354	109

Lapford station is situated on the line between Exeter St Davids and Barnstaple. The station serves the village of Lapford which lies to the north of the station.

First Great Western provide a service of four trains in each direction. 142001 pulls away from Lapford with the 17.09 Barnstaple-Exmouth on 16 June 2009.

Most services originate from Exmouth eleven miles south of Exeter St Davids. 142009/153308 arrive at Lapford with the 16.25 Exmouth-Barnstaple on 16 June 2009.

Britains Least Used Stations

KINGS NYMPTON

OPENED	1 AUGUST 1854
PRE GROUPING	LONDON & SOUTH WESTERN
MANAGED BY	FIRST GREAT WESTERN
PLATFORMS	1
REQUEST STOP	YES
SERVICE	MON-FRI SAT SUN
FREQUENCY	C C C

STATION USAGE	NUMBER OF PASSENGERS	LEAST USED
2008/09	1542	97
2009/10	1984	108
2010/11	2578	129
2011/12	3006	133
2012/13	4482	165
2013/14	3748	139

Kings Nympton station is situated on the Exeter St Davids-Barnstaple line 14 miles from Barnstaple. The station opened as South Molton Road and became Kings Nympton in 1951. The village of Kings Nympton is two miles from the station.

The station building is thought to be in private ownership.

Classes 142 143 and 150 DMUs. share duties on the line. 142029 pauses with the 8.43 Barnstaple-Exmouth on 16 June 2009. (below)

143603 arrives with the 7.51 Exmouth-Barnstaple on 11 June 2015. (below right)

Britains Least Used Stations

151

PORTSMOUTH ARMS

OPENED	1 AUGUST 1854
PRE GROUPING	LONDON & SOUTH WESTERN
MANAGED BY	FIRST GREAT WESTERN
PLATFORMS	1
REQUEST STOP	YES
SERVICE FREQUENCY	MON-FRI SAT SUN C C C

STATION USAGE	NUMBER OF PASSENGERS	LEAST USED
2008/09	844	55
2009/10	676	50
2010/11	936	55
2011/12	884	52
2012/13	694	45
2013/14	844	46

Portsmouth Arms station is on the Exeter St Davids-Barnstaple line eleven miles south of Barnstaple.

The station is situated on the A377 road between Exeter and Barnstaple and 200 yards from the Portsmouth Arms Public House after which the station was named.

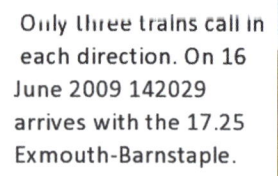

Only three trains call in each direction. On 16 June 2009 142029 arrives with the 17.25 Exmouth-Barnstaple.

CHAPELTON

OPENED	8 JUNE 1857
PRE GROUPING	LONDON & SOUTH WESTERN
MANAGED BY	FIRST GREAT WESTERN
PLATFORMS	1
REQUEST STOP	YES
SERVICE	MON-FRI SAT SUN
FREQUENCY	C C C

STATION USAGE	NUMBER OF PASSENGERS	LEAST USED
2008/09	176	14
2009/10	162	9
2010/11	190	19
2011/12	190	16
2012/13	258	21
2013/14	232	18

Chapelton is the final intermediate station on line from Exeter St Davids to Barnstaple. It is situated four and a half miles from Barnstaple and serves the small village of Chapelton.

The station building on the disused platform is in private ownership. The green Southern Railway sign is still retained.

Chapelton sees only one morning and one afternoon service towards Exeter. 142064 calls with the 7.09 Barnstaple- Exmouth on 16 June 2009.(below)

150221 is seen arriving on 11 June 2015 with the 6.14 Exmouth to Barnstaple. (below right)

Britains Least Used Stations

SAMPFORD COURTENAY

OPENED	8 JANUARY 1867
PRE GROUPING	LONDON & SOUTH WESTERN
MANAGED BY	DARTMOOR RAILWAY
PLATFORMS	1
REQUEST STOP	NO
SERVICE FREQUENCY	MON-FRI SAT SUN X X B (X SUNDAY WINTER)
STATION USAGE	NUMBER OF PASSENGERS / LEAST USED
2008/09	N/A
2009/10	N/A
2010/11	76 / 8
2011/12	136 / 12
2012/13	150 / 13
2013/14	146 / 14

Sampford Courtenay station is on the Dartmoor Line which branches off the Exeter St Davids-Barnstaple line just beyond Yeoford station. It is situated four miles from the terminus at Okehampton. The station was opened as Okehampton Road became Belstone Corner and finally Sampford Courtenay. In 1972 the station was closed. It was reopened in 2002 with a Sunday only service during the summer.

Usage figures are only available from 2010/11 and these figures show Sampford Courtenay to be one of the least used stations. On 14 June 2015 153380 is ready to depart with the 17.59 Okehampton-Exeter St Davids (right) and with the 16.29 Exeter St James-Okehampton. (below)

Britains Least Used Stations

OKEHAMPTON

OPENED	3 OCTOBER 1871
PRE GROUPING	LONDON & SOUTH WESTERN
MANAGED BY	DARTMOOR RAILWAY
PLATFORMS	2
REQUEST STOP	NO
SERVICE	MON-FRI SAT SUN
FREQUENCY	X X B
	(X SUNDAY WINTER)
STATION USAGE	NUMBER OF PASSENGERS / LEAST USED
2008/09	N/A
2009/10	N/A
2010/11	3622 / 150
2011/12	3526 / 143
2012/13	3438 / 142
2013/14	3208 / 131

Okehampton used to be a through station with services to Bude, Padstow and Plymouth via Tavistock. These lines were closed following the Beeching report in 1963 and Okehampton lost its services in 1972. The line remained open to Meldon Quarry thanks to freight and Okehampton reopened in 1997 but only on Sunday during the summer.

There are four services between Exeter and Okehampton on summer Sundays. 153380 stands in the platform to form the 17.59 service to Exeter St Davids on 14 June 2015.

Heritage DEMUs operate the two mile line to Meldon Quarry. 205032 is awaiting its next service on 16 July 2006. 150261 is seen alongside ready to leave with the 14.05 Okehampton-Exeter Central .

Britains Least Used Stations

KEYHAM

OPENED	2 JUNE 1900
PRE GROUPING	GREAT WESTERN
MANAGED BY	FIRST GREAT WESTERN
PLATFORMS	2
REQUEST STOP	NO
SERVICE	MON-FRI SAT SUN
FREQUENCY	B B B

STATION USAGE	NUMBER OF PASSENGERS	LEAST USED
2008/09	5600	201
2009/10	5016	184
2010/11	6330	205
2011/12	7700	218
2012/13	6540	197
2013/14	7100	205

Keyham station is situated on the Cornish Main Line three miles west of Plymouth. It serves the suburb of Keyham on the outskirts of the City.

First Great Western provides a two hourly service with trains to Gunnislake. On 17 July 2014 150130 is seen departing with the 12.54 from Plymouth.

On 17 July 2014 HST No 43053 with 43179 at the rear speeds through Keyham with the 10.06 Paddington- Penzance.

Britains Least Used Stations

COOMBE JUNCTION HALT

OPENED	15TH MAY 1901
PRE GROUPING	GREAT WESTERN
MANAGED BY	FIRST GREAT WESTERN
PLATFORMS	1
REQUEST STOP	NO
SERVICE	MON-FRI SAT SUN
FREQUENCY	C C X

STATION USAGE	NUMBER OF PASSENGERS	LEAST USED
2008/09	118	7
2009/10	42	1
2010/11	38	3
2011/12	60	5
2012/13	48	2
2013/14	42	5

Coombe Junction Halt is on the Looe Valley Line two miles from Liskeard. Approaching Coombe all trains have to reverse, but only two services continue the short distance to call at the station. Coombe is one of the least used stations. Only Teesside Airport had fewer passengers for 2012/13.

Only two stations retain the word Halt the other being St Keyne the following station on the line.

On 18 June 2013 153329 has arrived at Coombe with the 8.33 Liskeard-Looe. The driver has changed ends ready to continue the journey to Looe.(below)

On 17 July 2014 150122 enters Coombe on its return trip to Liskeard with the 9.09 service from Looe.(below right)

Britains Least Used Stations 157

ST. KEYNE WISHING WELL HALT

OPENED	1 SEPTEMBER 1902
PRE GROUPING	GREAT WESTERN
MANAGED BY	FIRST GREAT WESTERN
PLATFORMS	1
REQUEST STOP	YES
SERVICE	MON-FRI SAT SUN
FREQUENCY	B B B
	(X SUNDAY WINTER)
STATION	NUMBER OF LEAST
USAGE	PASSENGERS USED
2008/09	984 61
2009/10	936 57
2010/11	1072 62
2011/12	1062 58
2012/13	980 55
2013/14	1362 65

St Keyne Wishing Well Halt station is situated on the Looe Valley Line four miles from Liskeard. There is a small well half a mile from the station and the village of St Keyne is located one mile away.

St Keyne along with Coombe are the only stations to retain the word Halt.

First Great Western provide a service of ten trains in each direction. On 18 June 2013 153329 calls at St Keyne with the 9.58 Liskeard-Looe. (above right)

On the same date 153329 is seen from the overbridge with the 9.09 Looe- Liskeard.

Britains Least Used Stations

CAUSELAND

OPENED	11 SEPTEMBER 1879
PRE GROUPING	GREAT WESTERN
MANAGED BY	FIRST GREAT WESTERN
PLATFORMS	1
REQUEST STOP	YES
SERVICE	MON-FRI SAT SUN
FREQUENCY	B B B
	(X SUNDAY WINTER)
STATION	NUMBER OF LEAST
USAGE	PASSENGERS USED
2008/09	4014 168
2009/10	3652 152
2010/11	2674 131
2011/12	3366 139
2012/13	2544 120
2013/14	2198 104

Causeland station is situated on the Looe Valley Line five miles from Liskeard. It serves the village of Duloe one mile from the station.

150122 enters the station with the 7.46 Looe-Liskeard on 17 July 2014.

On 18 June 2013 153329 is ready to depart with the 9.58 Liskeard-Looe.

Britains Least Used Stations   159

SANDPLACE

OPENED	DECEMBER 1881
PRE GROUPING	GREAT WESTERN
MANAGED BY	FIRST GREAT WESTERN
PLATFORMS	1
REQUEST STOP	YES
SERVICE FREQUENCY	MON-FRI SAT SUN B B B (X SUNDAY WINTER)
STATION USAGE	NUMBER OF PASSENGERS / LEAST USED
2008/09	1142 / 73
2009/10	1148 / 68
2010/11	1032 / =59
2011/12	1422 / 75
2012/13	1486 / 70
2013/14	1860 / 88

Sandplace is the final intermediate station on the Looe Valley Line just over two miles from Looe. The village of Sandplace is situated half a mile from the station.

The station was known as Sandplace Halt between 1953 and 1969. Like many other stations the word Halt was removed in 1969 leaving only Coombe and St Keyne retaining the word Halt.

153329 arrives at Sandplace with the 9.09 Looe-Liskeard on 18 June 2013.

Britains Least Used Stations

LUXULYAN

OPENED	20 JUNE 1876
PRE GROUPING	GREAT WESTERN
MANAGED BY	FIRST GREAT WESTERN
PLATFORMS	1
REQUEST STOP	YES
SERVICE	MON-FRI SAT SUN
FREQUENCY	B B C
	(X SAT. SUMMER)
STATION	NUMBER OF LEAST
USAGE	PASSENGERS USED
2008/09	1210 78
2009/10	1372 74
2010/11	1420 72
2011/12	1836 94
2012/13	1428 67
2013/14	1654 79

Luxulyan station is the first of five intermediate stations on the Atlantic Coast Line between Par and Newquay. It is situated four miles from the Cornish Main Line at Par. The station was originally called Bridges and was renamed Luxulyan in 1905 after the village located to the east of the station.

The station formally had an island platform with a passing loop. This was removed in 1964.

First Great Western Class 150 DMUs provide services on the line. On 11 June 2015 150244 calls with the 19.24 Newquay-Par .(below)

150239 enters the station with the 14.03 Par-Newquay on 4 June 2010.(below right)

Britains Least Used Stations

BUGLE

OPENED	20 JUNE 1876
PRE GROUPING	GREAT WESTERN
MANAGED BY	FIRST GREAT WESTERN
PLATFORMS	1
REQUEST STOP	YES
SERVICE	MON-FRI SAT SUN
FREQUENCY	B B C
	(X SAT. SUMMER)
STATION USAGE	NUMBER OF PASSENGERS	LEAST USED
2008/09	2508	130
2009/10	3694	154
2010/11	3650	151
2011/12	5902	189
2012/13	6762	204
2013/14	6810	197

Bugle station is on the Atlantic Coast Line between Par and Newquay and serves the village of Bugle situated south of the station.

On 11 June 2015 150244 pauses with the 17.22 Newquay-Par.

The number of passengers using Bugle has been steadily increasing and it is now easily the busiest intermediate station on the line. 150239 calls to pick up passengers with the 16.10 Par-Newquay on 4 June 2010.

162   *Britains Least Used Stations*

ROCHE

OPENED	20 JUNE 1876
PRE GROUPING	GREAT WESRERN
MANAGED BY	FIRST GREAT WESTERN
PLATFORMS	1
REQUEST STOP	YES
SERVICE	MON-FRI SAT SUN
FREQUENCY	B B C
	(X SAT SUMMER)
STATION	NUMBER OF LEAST
USAGE	PASSENGERS USED
2008/09	1214 79
2009/10	1570 84
2010/11	2144 109
2011/12	2720 124
2012/13	1700 84
2013/14	1950 93

Roche station is on the Atlantic Coast Line between Par and Newquay nine miles from Par. The station was originally called Victoria but was renamed Roche in 1904. The station is situated in the village of Victoria with the larger village of Roche one mile south of the station.

The line has a service of five or six trains in each direction on Monday to Saturday with three each way on Sunday. However on peak summer Saturdays there is no service for any intermediate station as the line is worked to full capacity by through trains bringing holidaymakers to Newquay. 150244 pauses with the 18.29 Par-Newquay on 11 June 2015

On 4 June 2010 150239 calls with the 14.58 Newquay-Par.

Britains Least Used Stations

ST COLUMB ROAD

OPENED	20 JUNE 1876
PRE GROUPING	GREAT WESTERN
MANAGED BY	FIRST GREAT WESTERN
PLATFORMS	1
REQUEST STOP	YES
SERVICE	MON-FRI SAT SUN
FREQUENCY	B B C
	(X SAT SUMMER)
STATION	NUMBER OF LEAST
USAGE	PASSENGERS USED
2008/09	1148	76
2009/10	1590	86
2010/11	1966	100
2011/12	1792	91
2012/13	1548	74
2013/14	2188	103

St Columb Road station is situated on the Atlantic Coast Line six miles south of Newquay. The nearest village is Indian Queens one mile away on the main A30 road. The village of St. Columb Major is situated over two miles north of the station.

After a torrential downpour 150244 arrives into St Columb Road on 11 June 2015 with the 17.22 Newquay-Par.

On 4 June 2010 150239 calls with the 10.13 Newquay-Par.

Britains Least Used Stations

QUINTREL DOWNS

OPENED	2 OCTOBER 1911
PRE GROUPING	GREAT WESTERN
MANAGED BY	FIRST GREAT WESTERN
PLATFORMS	1
REQUEST STOP	YES
SERVICE	MON-FRI SAT SUN
FREQUENCY	B B C
	(X SAT SUMMER)
STATION USAGE	NUMBER OF PASSENGERS / LEAST USED
2008/09	526 / =37
2009/10	974 / =60
2010/11	1270 / 69
2011/12	1304 / 67
2012/13	814 / 50
2013/14	1286 / 60

Quintrel Downs is the last intermediate station on the Atlantic Coast Line two and a half miles from Newquay. It was originally known as Quintrel Downs Platform. The word platform was dropped in 1956.

150239 stands in the platform with the 12.11 Par-Newquay on 4 June 2010.

With just two minutes turnaround time allowed at Newquay 150239 is entering Quintrel Downs on its return journey with the 13.03 from Newquay.

Britains Least Used Stations

LELANT

OPENED	1 JUNE 1877
PRE GROUPING	GREAT WESTERN
MANAGED BY	FIRST GREAT WESTERN
PLATFORMS	1
REQUEST STOP	YES
SERVICE	MON-FRI SAT SUN
FREQUENCY	C C C

STATION USAGE	NUMBER OF PASSENGERS	LEAST USED
2008/09	560	43
2009/10	324	28
2010/11	1842	94
2011/12	2908	130
2012/13	2322	112
2013/14	2494	113

Lelant station is on the picturesque St Ives Bay Line between St Erth and St Ives. It is situated on the western shore line of the estuary of the River Hayle. The station serves the village of Lelant. A park and ride station was opened in 1978 at Lelant Saltings half a mile away to ease traffic congestion in St Ives.

Another view looking towards St Ives with a four coach train approaching Lelant on 2 June 2006.

Services are provided by First Great Western. During the summer months the line is very busy. Four coaches are required to meet the demand of holidaymakers travelling to the delightful resort of St Ives. On 22 July 2013 150221/202 are seen with the 10.13 St Erth-St Ives.

166 Britains Least Used Stations

LONGCROSS

OPENED	21 SEPTEMBER 1942
PRE GROUPING	N/A
MANAGED BY	SOUTH WEST TRAINS
PLATFORMS	2
REQUEST STOP	NO
SERVICE	MON-FRI SAT SUN
FREQUENCY	B X X

STATION USAGE	NUMBER OF PASSENGERS	LEAST USED
2008/09	7596	234
2009/10	9650	261
2010/11	10686	269
2011/12	12324	282
2012/13	5086	174
2013/14	10044	244

Longcross station is on the Waterloo to Reading Line between Virginia Water and Sunningdale. It is situated one mile from the village of Longcross adjacent to a military instillation. Longcross is not accessible by vehicles but only along a path from the village.

Longcross is served by South West Trains mainly during morning and afternoon peaks. Currently these services are in the hands of Class 458 Juniper units. 8026/8020 approach the station with the 12.50 Waterloo-Reading on 19 March 2014.

On 17 June 2009 450083 passes through the station with the 7.54 Richmond- Guildford.

Britains Least Used Stations

PEVENSEY BAY

OPENED	11 SEPTEMBER 1905
PRE GROUPING	LONDON, BRIGHTON & SOUTH COAST
MANAGED BY	SOUTHERN
PLATFORMS	2
REQUEST STOP	NO
SERVICE FREQUENCY	MON-FRI SAT SUN
	C X X

STATION USAGE	NUMBER OF PASSENGERS	LEAST USED
2008/09	3902	164
2009/10	4010	165
2010/11	3438	147
2011/12	3634	146
2012/13	5214	177
2013/14	6838	199

Pevensey Bay station is on the line between Eastbourne and Hastings. It is situated near the coast one mile east of Pevensey and Westham station. There is no immediate settlement near the station.

Pevensey Bay receives a limited service operated by Southern. 377152 is seen departing with the 7.38 Hastings-Victoria on 12 June 2015. This is the only westbound morning service from the station. (right)

377107 calls with the 7.38 Eastbourne- Ore on 12 June 2015 the first of two eastbound services in the morning. (below)

On 13 June 2008 171722 passes at speed with the 7.22 Brighton -Ashford International. (below right)

168

Britains Least Used Stations

THREE OAKS

OPENED	1 JULY 1907
PRE GROUPING	SOUTH EASTERN & CHATHAM
MANAGED BY	SOUTHERN
PLATFORMS	1
REQUEST STOP	NO
SERVICE	MON-FRI SAT SUN
FREQUENCY	B B C

STATION USAGE	NUMBER OF PASSENGERS	LEAST USED
2008/09	504	35
2009/10	532	42
2010/11	1540	79
2011/12	6088	194
2012/13	5438	181
2013/14	6912	200

Three Oaks station is situated on the line between Hastings and Ashford International. The station opened as Three Oaks Bridge Halt then became Three Oaks and Guestling and finally Three Oaks in 1980. Until December 2010 Three Oaks only received a limited peak hour service. Now with a regular two hourly service the number of passengers has shown an increase from 500 to over 6000.

Southern provide the services using Class 171 DMUs. 171730 arrives with the 10.33 Ashford International -Brighton on 12 June 2015.

171728 calls with the 11.32 Brighton-Ashford International on 13 May 2011.

Britains Least Used Stations 169

WINCHELSEA

OPENED	13 FEBRUARY 1851
PRE GROUPING	SOUTH EASTERN
MANAGED BY	SOUTHERN
PLATFORMS	1
REQUEST STOP	NO
SERVICE FREQUENCY	MON-FRI SAT SUN B B C

STATION USAGE	NUMBER OF PASSENGERS	LEAST USED
2008/09	1090	67
2009/10	974	=60
2010/11	474	38
2011/12	4878	171
2012/13	6798	205
2013/14	6640	195

Winchelsea station is on the Marshlink Line between Hastings and Ashford International. The station is situated two miles south west of Rye and serves the town of Winchelsea half a mile south east of the station.

Winchelsea along with the neighbouring stations at Doleham and Three Oaks has received a much improved service since 2011. The increase in passenger numbers at Winchelsea is particularly noticeable. 171730 departs with the 8.32 Brighton-Ashford International on 12 June 2015.

On 13 May 2011 171728 calls with the 9.33 Ashford International-Brighton.

SWALE

OPENED	1 MARCH 1923
PRE GROUPING	SOUTHERN
MANAGED BY	SOUTH EASTERN
PLATFORMS	1
REQUEST STOP	NO
SERVICE	MON-FRI SAT SUN
FREQUENCY	A A A

STATION USAGE	NUMBER OF PASSENGERS	LEAST USED
2008/09	2394	=126
2009/10	2876	140
2010/11	4068	166
2011/12	5996	190
2012/13	3372	140
2013/14	3792	140

Swale station is on the eight mile branch line between Sittingbourne and Sheerness-on-Sea and is situated just before the line crosses the Swale into the Isle of Sheppey. The station was opened as Kings Ferry Bridge Halt and renamed Swale in 1929. When the new road bridge was built in 1960 the station was resited. There is no settlement near the station but it still receives an excellent service of a train every half hour. (every hour on Sunday)

Despite the low number of passengers using the station it has an indicator board showing the times of trains. The elevated road which crosses the Swale can be seen on the left of the picture with the rail bridge visible in the distance.(right)

Services are provided by Southeastern. 466037 arrives with the 13.21 Sheerness-on Sea-Sittingbourne on 3 June 2015. (below)

On 7 July 2012 466008 calls with the 11.40 Sittingbourne-Sheerness-on- Sea. (below right)

Britains Least Used Stations   171

BARRHILL

OPENED	5 OCTOBER 1877
PRE GROUPING	GLASGOW & SOUTH WESTERN
MANAGED BY	SCOTRAIL
PLATFORMS	2
REQUEST STOP	NO
SERVICE FREQUENCY	MON-FRI SAT SUN B B C

STATION USAGE	NUMBER OF PASSENGERS	LEAST USED
2008/09	4864	189
2009/10	4568	179
2010/11	4804	182
2011/12	5290	181
2012/13	5712	189
2013/14	11214	259

Barrhill station is on the line between Glasgow Central and Stranraer. The nearest stations are Girvan 14 miles to the north and Stranraer 26 miles to the south. The village of Barrhill is located one mile from the station. The number of passengers using the station for 2013/4 has doubled from previous years.

Scotrail provide class 156 DMUs for services on the line with six trains in each direction on weekdays. 156511 is ready to depart with the 9.38 Glasgow Central-Stranaer on 17 June 2014.

Barrhill provides a passing place for a line which is single between Ayr and Stranraer. 156511 is seen returning with the 12.50 Stranraer -Glasgow Central while 156496 heads south with the 11.50 Glasgow Central-Stranraer on 17 June 2014.

Britains Least Used Stations

BREICH

OPENED	9 JULY 1869
PRE GROUPING	CALEDONIAN
MANAGED BY	SCOTRAIL
PLATFORMS	2
REQUEST STOP	NO
SERVICE	MON-FRI SAT SUN
FREQUENCY	D D X

STATION USAGE	NUMBER OF PASSENGERS	LEAST USED
2008/09	200	=15
2009/10	116	6
2010/11	68	=5
2011/12	90	8
2012/13	102	8
2013/14	64	6

Breich station is situated on the Edinburgh Waverley to Glasgow Central via Shotts Line 21 miles west of Edinburgh. The station serves the small village of Breich. With less than 100 passengers using the station Breich is currently the second least used station in Scotland.

The line sees a regular hourly service but only one train in each direction call at Breich. There is a morning service to Edinburgh and an evening service to Glasgow. 156507 is seen on this service the 17.52 Edinburgh-Glasgow Central on 25 August 2008.

On the same date a pair of Class 156 DMUs headed by 156462 hurry through Breich with the 17.21 Edinburgh-Glasgow Central.

Britains Least Used Stations

SPRINGFIELD

OPENED	20 SEPTEMBER 1847
PRE GROUPING	NORTH BRITISH
MANAGED BY	SCOTRAIL
PLATFORMS	2
REQUEST STOP	NO
SERVICE	MON-FRI SAT SUN
FREQUENCY	C C X

STATION USAGE	NUMBER OF PASSENGERS	LEAST USED
2008/09	680	50
2009/10	860	56
2010/11	708	49
2011/12	772	48
2012/13	646	41
2013/14	680	40

Springfield station is on the line between Edinburgh and Aberdeen 17 miles south of Dundee. It serves the village of Springfield situated west of the station. Note how part of the station has a very low platform.

Only three trains in each direction call at Springfield. 170450/158711 arrive with the 8.00 Edinburgh-Dundee on 16 June 2015.

On the 12 June 2009 158706/170723 call with the 17.03 Edinburgh-Carnoustie.

Britains Least Used Stations

INVERGOWRIE

OPENED	24 MAY 1847
PRE GROUPING	CALEDONIAN
MANAGED BY	SCOTRAIL
PLATFORMS	2
REQUEST STOP	NO
SERVICE	MON-FRI SAT SUN
FREQUENCY	B B X

STATION USAGE	NUMBER OF PASSENGERS	LEAST USED
2008/09	1144	74
2009/10	1758	94
2010/11	2078	105
2011/12	2338	112
2012/13	2980	133
2013/14	4674	165

Invergowrie station is on the Glasgow Queen Street to Aberdeen line three and a half miles west of Dundee. The station serves the village of Invergowrie situated on the north bank of the Firth of Tay.

Invergowrie has seen a steady rise in passenger numbers with a service of six trains in each direction mainly at peak times. On 16 June 2015 170450 arrives with the 15.33 Aberdeen-Glasgow Queen Street.

With the skyline of Dundee in the background 170401 hurries through the station with the 13.42 Aberdeen-Glasgow Queen Street on 12 June 2009.

Britains Least Used Stations

BALMOSSIE

OPENED	18 JUNE 1962
PRE GROUPING	N/A
MANAGED BY	SCOTRAIL
PLATFORMS	2 (STAGGERED)
REQUEST STOP	NO
SERVICE	MON-FRI SAT SUN
FREQUENCY	D D X

STATION USAGE	NUMBER OF PASSENGERS	LEAST USED
2008/09	406	32
2009/10	804	55
2010/11	362	30
2011/12	314	25
2012/13	1078	61
2013/14	1446	73

Balmossie station is on the line between Dundee and Aberdeen six miles north east of Dundee. Opened as Balmossie Halt the halt was dropped in 1983. Balmossie receives only one early morning service to Dundee and one in the evening to Carnoustie.

Scotrail Class 170 Turbostars are employed with services on the line. 170431 speeds through Balmossie with the 9.41 Glasgow Queen Street - Aberdeen on 12 June 2009.

On 16 June 2015 170402 heads south with the 9.07 Dyce-Glasgow Queen Street.

Britains Least Used Stations

MONIFIETH

OPENED	8 OCTOBER 1838
PRE GROUPING	DUNDEE & ARBROATH
MANAGED BY	SCOTRAIL
PLATFORMS	2
REQUEST STOP	NO
SERVICE	MON-FRI SAT SUN
FREQUENCY	C C X

STATION USAGE	NUMBER OF PASSENGERS	LEAST USED
2008/09	2082	115
2009/10	1170	69
2010/11	1288	70
2011/12	2398	113
2012/13	2570	122
2013/14	3122	127

Monifieth station is situated on the line between Dundee and Aberdeen six and a half miles north east of Dundee. It serves the town of Monifieth which has a population of over 8,000. For a town of its size it is somewhat surprising that it receives such a poor service of only three trains in each direction.

A HST hurries through Monifieth with the 7.10 Leeds-Aberdeen on 16 June 2015.

On 12 June 2009 170425 heads towards Glasgow Queen Street with the 8.29 service from Aberdeen.

Britains Least Used Stations 177

BARRY LINKS

OPENED	JULY 1851
PRE GROUPING	DUNDEE & ARBROATH
MANAGED BY	SCOTRAIL
PLATFORMS	2
REQUEST STOP	NO
SERVICE	MON-FRI SAT SUN
FREQUENCY	D D X

STATION USAGE	NUMBER OF PASSENGERS	LEAST USED
2008/09	94	5
2009/10	90	4
2010/11	74	7
2011/12	86	7
2012/13	52	4
2013/14	42	4

Barry Links station is on the line between Dundee and Aberdeen one and a quarter miles south west of Carnoustie. It serves the village of Barry situated half a mile north of the station. The station opened as Barry and was renamed Barry Links in 1919.

Barry Links is the least used station in Scotland with less than 100 passengers using the station each year. A Class 170 Turbostar is seen passing with the 7.30 Edinburgh-Inverurie on 12 June 2009.

Another Class 170 170429 speeds through the station with the 11.42 Aberdeen-Glasgow Queen Street on 16 June 2015.

178   Britains Least Used Stations

GOLF STREET

OPENED	7 NOVEMBER 1960
PRE GROUPING	N/A
MANAGED BY	SCOTRAIL
PLATFORMS	2
REQUEST STOP	NO
SERVICE	MON-FRI SAT SUN
FREQUENCY	D D X

STATION USAGE	NUMBER OF PASSENGERS	LEAST USED
2008/09	136	11
2009/10	190	13
2010/11	122	14
2011/12	212	19
2012/13	112	9
2013/14	90	9

Golf Street station is on the line between Dundee and Aberdeen half a mile south west of Carnoustie. The station was opened as Golf Street Halt the halt being dropped in 1983. Carnoustie Golf Course is situated close to the station.

Golf Street like Balmossie and Barry Links receives just one service in each direction. On 20 July 2012 170473 calls with the 17.11 Glasgow Queen Street-Carnoustie.

On the same date 170406 hurries through the station with the 17.37 Edinburgh-Aberdeen.

Britains Least Used Stations

DALWHINNIE

OPENED	9 SEPTEMBER 1863
PRE GROUPING	HIGHLAND RAILWAY
MANAGED BY	SCOTRAIL
PLATFORMS	2
REQUEST STOP	NO
SERVICE	MON-FRI SAT SUN
FREQUENCY	C C C

STATION USAGE	NUMBER OF PASSENGERS	LEAST USED
2008/09	2296	122
2009/10	2208	120
2010/11	1894	96
2011/12	1984	99
2012/13	2172	103
2013/14	2472	112

Dalwhinnie station is situated on the Highland Main Line midway between Perth and Inverness. The station serves the small village of Dalwhinnie famous for its whisky distillery. The highest point on the rail network is to be found just south of the station although Corrour on the West Highland Line is the highest station.

All services are provided by class 170 Turbostars. 170412 speeds past Dalwhinnie with the 7.55 Inverness-Edinburgh on 12 June 2007.

Dalwhinnie receives six northbound and four southbound services. On 20 July 2012 170427 calls with the 7.06 Glasgow Queen Street-Inverness.

Britains Least Used Stations

CARRBRIDGE

OPENED	8 JULY 1892
PRE GROUPING	HIGHLAND RAILWAY
MANAGED BY	SCOTRAIL
PLATFORMS	2
REQUEST STOP	NO
SERVICE	MON-FRI SAT SUN
FREQUENCY	C C C

STATION USAGE	NUMBER OF PASSENGERS	LEAST USED
2008/09	3796	157
2009/10	4500	178
2010/11	5118	187
2011/12	5636	187
2012/13	4454	164
2013/14	5540	182

Carrbridge station is situated on the Highland Main Line between Perth and Inverness seven miles north of Aviemore. The station serves the village of Carrbridge.

Scotrail provide a service of five trains in each direction. 170424 is seen arriving with the 9.18 Inverness-Glasgow Queen Street on 8 June 2010.(below)

On the same date HST No 43310 hurries past Carrbridge with the 7.55 Inverness-Kings Cross .(below right)

Britains Least Used Stations

GARELOCHHEAD

OPENED	7 AUGUST 1894
PRE GROUPING	NORTH BRITISH
MANAGED BY	SCOTRAIL
PLATFORMS	2 (ISLAND)
REQUEST STOP	NO
SERVICE	MON-FRI SAT SUN
FREQUENCY	B B C

STATION USAGE	NUMBER OF PASSENGERS	LEAST USED
2008/09	5374	197
2009/10	4706	181
2010/11	5040	184
2011/12	5122	176
2012/13	5682	188
2013/14	5256	178

Garelochhead station is on the West Highland Line 32 miles from Glasgow Queen Street. The station serves the village of Garelochhead which is situated at the northern end of Gare Loch.

The large island platform is typical of a number of stations on the West Highland Line.

Services are provided by Scotrail Class 156 DMUs. 156474/476 arrive with the 12.56 Oban-Glasgow Queen Street on 31 August 2010.

182

Britains Least Used Stations

ARDLUI

OPENED	7 AUGUST 1894
PRE GROUPING	NORTH BRITISH
MANAGED BY	SCOTRAIL
PLATFORMS	2 (ISLAND)
REQUEST STOP	NO
SERVICE	MON-FRI SAT SUN
FREQUENCY	C C C

STATION USAGE	NUMBER OF PASSENGERS	LEAST USED
2008/09	2212	119
2009/10	1970	=106
2010/11	2092	107
2011/12	2260	=110
2012/13	2216	105
2013/14	4566	160

Ardlui station is situated on the West Highland Line 51 miles north of Glasgow and eight miles from Crianlarich where the Oban and Fort William lines divide. The station serves the hamlet of Ardlui which is located at the head of Loch Lomond. The number of passengers using the station has doubled in 2013/14.

On 31 August 2010 a six coach train formed of 156457/447/496 is ready to depart with the 10.10 Mallaig and 12.11 Oban-Glasgow Queen Street while 156458/453 head north with the 12.21 Glasgow Queen Street-Oban and Mallaig.

Britains Least Used Stations

TYNDRUM LOWER

OPENED	1 AUGUST 1873
PRE GROUPING	CALEDONIAN
MANAGED BY	SCOTRAIL
PLATFORMS	1
REQUEST STOP	NO
SERVICE	MON-FRI SAT SUN
FREQUENCY	C C C

STATION USAGE	NUMBER OF PASSENGERS	LEAST USED
2008/09	4552	179
2009/10	4146	170
2010/11	3856	158
2011/12	3698	147
2012/13	3928	=153
2013/14	4082	147

Tyndrum Lower station is on the Oban branch of the West Highland Line five miles from Crianlarich. The station opened as Tyndrum with the lower added in 1956. The village of Tyndrum has a second station Upper Tyndrum half a mile away on the Fort William Line.

A four coach train would have split at Crianlarich with two coaches going forward to Fort William and two going to Oban. 156450 arrives at Tyndrum Lower with the 12.21 Glasgow Queen Street-Oban on 11 July 2014.

The same unit is seen on its return journey to Glasgow Queen Street with the 18.11 service from Oban.

Britains Least Used Stations

DALMALLY

OPENED	1 APRIL 1877
PRE GROUPING	CALEDONIAN
MANAGED BY	SCOTRAIL
PLATFORMS	2
REQUEST STOP	NO
SERVICE	MON-FRI SAT SUN
FREQUENCY	C C C

STATION USAGE	NUMBER OF PASSENGERS	LEAST USED
2008/09	4128	170
2009/10	4046	166
2010/11	4696	180
2011/12	3604	145
2012/13	4534	167
2013/14	4632	163

Dalmally station is situated on the Oban branch of the West Highland Line. It serves the village of Dalmally which is located three miles east of the head of Loch Awe.

The station building appears to be in private ownership.

In addition to the Glasgow Queen Street Oban services there is an afternoon service between Oban and Dalmally. On 11 July 2014 156450 has arrived with the 16.11 Oban- Dalmally and will form the 17.05 return to Oban.

Britains Least Used Stations

LOCH AWE

OPENED	1 JULY 1880
PRE GROUPING	CALEDONIAN
MANAGED BY	SCOTRAIL
PLATFORMS	1
REQUEST STOP	NO
SERVICE	MON-FRI SAT SUN
FREQUENCY	C C C

STATION USAGE	NUMBER OF PASSENGERS	LEAST USED
2008/09	2526	131
2009/10	2926	142
2010/11	3160	143
2011/12	2544	118
2012/13	2716	125
2013/14	3034	126

Loch Awe station is on the Oban branch of the West Highland Line. The station is situated on the northern banks of Loch Awe and serves a small community and a hotel adjacent to the station.

An old Mark 1 carriage stands at the west of the station. It arrived in 1988 and was used as a tea room until 2008.

On 11 July 2014 156456 calls with the 14.41 Oban -Glasgow Queen Street.

Britains Least Used Stations

FALLS OF CRUACHAN

OPENED	1 OCTOBER 1893	
PRE GROUPING	CALEDONIAN	
MANAGED BY	SCOTRAIL	
PLATFORMS	1	
REQUEST STOP	YES	
SERVICE	MON-FRI SAT SUN	
FREQUENCY	C C C	
	(NO WINTER SERVICE)	
STATION USAGE	NUMBER OF PASSENGERS	LEAST USED
2008/09	218	=21
2009/10	204	=15
2010/11	200	=20
2011/12	250	23
2012/13	244	20
2013/14	498	31

Falls of Cruachan station is on the Oban branch of the West Highland Line 18 miles from Oban. The station is situated near to the Cruachan Dam hydro-electric power station at the foot of Ben Cruachan. The station was closed between 1965 and 1988 and is now only opened during summer months.

The station is well cared for the platform being lined with tubs containing flowers and plants.

156476/450 arrive at Falls of Cruachan with the 12.11 Oban-Glasgow Queen Street on 7 July 2011.

Britains Least Used Stations 187

CONNEL FERRY

OPENED	1 JULY 1880
PRE GROUPING	CALEDONIAN
MANAGED BY	SCOTRAIL
PLATFORMS	1
REQUEST STOP	NO
SERVICE	MON-FRI SAT SUN
FREQUENCY	C C C

STATION USAGE	NUMBER OF PASSENGERS	LEAST USED
2008/09	4330	177
2009/10	4088	168
2010/11	4056	165
2011/12	4316	162
2012/13	4004	157
2013/14	4400	156

Connel Ferry station is on the Oban branch of the West Highland Line six miles from Oban. The station serves the village of Connel which is situated on the southern shore of Loch Etive. Connel Ferry used to have an additional island platform and was the junction for a line to Ballachulish. The branch was closed in 1966 and the disused island platform demolished in 1985.

On 11 July 2014 156450 stands in the platform with the 17.05 Dalmally-Oban.

On the same date 156450 is seen arriving with the 18.11 Oban-Crianlarich.

188   Britains Least Used Stations

UPPER TYNDRUM

OPENED	7 AUGUST 1894
PRE GROUPING	NORTH BRITISH
MANAGED BY	SCOTRAIL
PLATFORMS	2 (ISLAND)
REQUEST STOP	NO
SERVICE	MON-FRI SAT SUN
FREQUENCY	C C C

STATION USAGE	NUMBER OF PASSENGERS	LEAST USED
2008/09	3488	153
2009/10	3680	153
2010/11	3784	156
2011/12	3472	140
2012/13	3396	141
2013/14	3940	144

Upper Tyndrum station is on The West Highland Line between Glasgow Queen Street and Fort William. It is situated five miles north of Crianlarich where the Oban Line divided. Tyndrum has a second station Tyndrum Lower on the Oban Line which is more conveniently located for the village.

The station opened as Tyndrum became Tyndrum Upper in 1956 and finally Upper Tyndrum in 1988.

On 11 July 2014 156465/499 are ready to leave with the 10.10 Mallaig -Glasgow Queen Street.

Britains Least Used Stations　　　　　　　　　　　　　　　　　　　　　　　　　　　189

BRIDGE OF ORCHY

OPENED	7 AUGUST 1894
PRE GROUPING	NORTH BRITISH
MANAGED BY	SCOTRAIL
PLATFORMS	2 (ISLAND)
REQUEST STOP	NO
SERVICE	MON-FRI SAT SUN
FREQUENCY	C C C

STATION USAGE	NUMBER OF PASSENGERS	LEAST USED
2008/09	5690	205
2009/10	5416	191
2010/11	6192	202
2011/12	5890	188
2012/13	5726	190
2013/14	5932	189

Bridge of Orchy station is on the West Highland Line 72 miles from Glasgow. The station serves the village of Bridge of Orchy situated south of Loch Tulla.

The station buildings are used as a bunkhouse for those walking the West Highland Way. 156465 stands in the platform with the 6.05 Mallaig-Glasgow Queen Street on 25 September 2007.

Stations on the West Highland Line have a direct service to London using the Caledonian Sleeper. This service runs every night except Saturday. On 11 July 2014 67007 pulls into Bridge of Orchy with the 19.50 Fort William-Euston Sleeper.

190   Britains Least Used Stations

TULLOCH

OPENED	7 AUGUST 1894
PRE GROUPING	NORTH BRITISH
MANAGED BY	SCOTRAIL
PLATFORMS	2
REQUEST STOP	NO
SERVICE	MON-FRI SAT SUN
FREQUENCY	C C C

STATION USAGE	NUMBER OF PASSENGERS	LEAST USED
2008/09	2394	=126
2009/10	2052	112
2010/11	2216	111
2011/12	2136	106
2012/13	2124	101
2013/14	2046	98

Tulloch station is situated on the West Highland Line 18 miles from Fort William. The station was originally called Inverlair after a village one mile from the station.

Like many stations on The West Highland Line the station building has been converted into a hostel for bunkhouse accommodation.

Tulloch has three services in each direction between Glasgow Queen Street and Mallaig plus the sleeper service between Euston and Fort William. On 11 July 2014 156500/447 call at Tulloch with the 8.21 Glasgow Queen Street -Mallaig.

Britains Least Used Stations 191

ROY BRIDGE

OPENED	7 AUGUST 1894
PRE GROUPING	NORTH BRITISH
MANAGED BY	SCOTRAIL
PLATFORMS	1
REQUEST STOP	NO
SERVICE	MON-FRI SAT SUN
FREQUENCY	C C C

STATION USAGE	NUMBER OF PASSENGERS	LEAST USED
2008/09	3936	165
2009/10	4112	169
2010/11	3878	159
2011/12	4084	155
2012/13	4270	159
2013/14	3856	142

Roy Bridge station is situated on the West Highland Line 12 miles from Fort William. The station serves the small village of Roy Bridge. The station once had two platforms but in 1966 the up platform was removed and the station buildings destroyed.

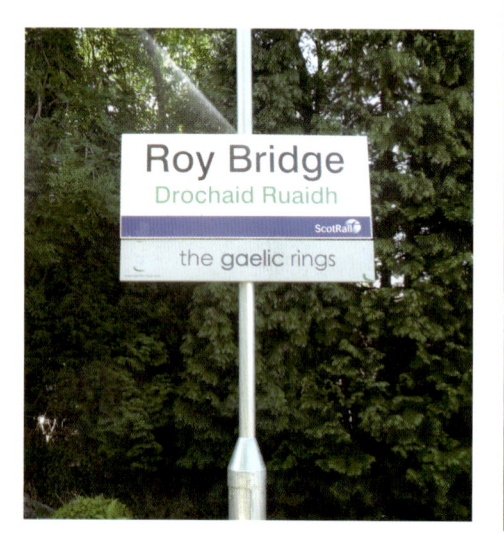

With the disused platform clearly visible 156465/499 arrive at Roy Bridge with the 10.10 Mallaig-Glasgow Queen Street on 11 July 2014.

On the same date 156500/447 head towards Fort William with the 8.21 Glasgow Queen Street-Mallaig.

Britains Least Used Stations

SPEAN BRIDGE

OPENED	7 AUGUST 1894
PRE GROUPING	NORTH BRITISH
MANAGED BY	SCOTRAIL
PLATFORMS	2
REQUEST STOP	NO
SERVICE	MON-FRI SAT SUN
FREQUENCY	C C C

STATION USAGE	NUMBER OF PASSENGERS	LEAST USED
2008/09	6570	222
2009/10	6312	209
2010/11	6386	207
2011/12	6960	207
2012/13	6558	200
2013/14	6808	196

Spean Bridge is the final station on the West Highland Line before reaching Fort William. The station serves the village of Spean Bridge. There was once a branch line which ran from Spean Bridge along the banks of Loch Lochy to Fort Augustus on the southern tip of Loch Ness. This line closed in 1933.

The former station building has been converted into a high class restaurant.

In 1987 the crossing loop was altered to right hand running. On 8 July 2011 156456 arrives with the 16.05 Mallaig-Glasgow Queen Street.

Britains Least Used Stations

BANAVIE

OPENED	1 APRIL 1901
PRE GROUPING	NORTH BRITISH
MANAGED BY	SCOTRAIL
PLATFORMS	1
REQUEST STOP	NO
SERVICE	MON-FRI SAT SUN
FREQUENCY	C C C

STATION USAGE	NUMBER OF PASSENGERS	LEAST USED
2008/09	4208	175
2009/10	4478	177
2010/11	5056	186
2011/12	5328	183
2012/13	6542	198
2013/14	5672	185

Banavie station is situated on the Mallaig extension of the West Highland Line two miles north of Fort William. The station serves the villages of Banavie and Caol.

A view of the signal box and the swing bridge over the Caledonian Canal with Ben Nevis in the background.

There are four trains in each direction between Fort William and Mallaig. In fading light 156485 is ready to leave Banavie with the 18.15 Mallaig-Fort William on 7 July 2011. This is the last service from Mallaig and connects with the Caledonian Sleeper service at Fort William.

194 Britains Least Used Stations

CORPACH

OPENED	1 APRIL 1901
PRE GROUPING	NORTH BRITISH
MANAGED BY	SCOTRAIL
PLATFORMS	1
REQUEST STOP	NO
SERVICE	MON-FRI SAT SUN
FREQUENCY	C C C

STATION USAGE	NUMBER OF PASSENGERS	LEAST USED
2008/09	2262	121
2009/10	2278	122
2010/11	2554	128
2011/12	2660	121
2012/13	2774	127
2013/14	2532	114

Corpach station is on the Mallaig extension of the West Highland Line three miles from Fort William. It serves the village of Corpach which is situated at the eastern end of Loch Eil.

A view looking in a westerly direction with the station exit at the end of the platform by the level crossing.

On 7 July 2011 156492/457 stand in the platform with the 16.05 Mallaig-Glasgow Queen Street.

Britains Least Used Stations 195

LOCH EIL OUTWARD BOUND

OPENED	6 MAY 1985
PRE GROUPING	N/A
MANAGED BY	SCOTRAIL
PLATFORMS	1
REQUEST STOP	NO
SERVICE	MON-FRI SAT SUN
FREQUENCY	C C C

STATION USAGE	NUMBER OF PASSENGERS	LEAST USED
2008/09	860	56
2009/10	548	44
2010/11	812	52
2011/12	722	=46
2012/13	578	37
2013/14	522	33

Loch Eil Outward Bound station is on the Mallaig extension of the West Highland Line six miles from Fort William. The station is situated on the northern bank of Loch Eil. The station was opened in 1985 to serve the nearby Outward Bound Centre.

156465/485 are seen departing with the 10.10 Mallaig-Glasgow Queen Street on 8 July 2011.

196

Britains Least Used Stations

LOCHEILSIDE

OPENED	1 APRIL 1901
PRE GROUPING	NORTH BRITISH
MANAGED BY	SCOTRAIL
PLATFORMS	1
REQUEST STOP	YES
SERVICE	MON-FRI SAT SUN
FREQUENCY	C C C
STATION	NUMBER OF LEAST
USAGE	PASSENGERS USED
2008/09	324 28
2009/10	268 =19
2010/11	372 31
2011/12	388 33
2012/13	488 35
2013/14	588 36

Locheilside station is on the Mallaig extension of the West Highland Line ten miles from Fort William. It is situated on the north bank of Loch Eil and serves a small number of houses along the banks of the Loch.

The station entrance taken from the A380 Fort William to Mallaig road with Loch Eil just visible behind the trees.

156485 is seen at Locheilside with the 12.21 Glasgow Queen Street-Mallaig on 7 July 2011.

Britains Least Used Stations

LOCHAILORT

OPENED	1 APRIL 1901
PRE GROUPING	NORTH BRITISH
MANAGED BY	SCOTRAIL
PLATFORMS	1
REQUEST STOP	YES
SERVICE	MON-FRI SAT SUN
FREQUENCY	C C C

STATION USAGE	NUMBER OF PASSENGERS	LEAST USED
2008/09	1658	99
2009/10	2102	=115
2010/11	2146	110
2011/12	2830	127
2012/13	2830	129
2013/14	2186	102

Lochailort station is on the Mallaig extension of the West Highland Line 16 miles from Mallaig. The station serves the village of Lochailort which is situated at the north east corner of Loch Ailort.

A view looking towards Fort William

On 8 July 2011 six passengers are waiting to board the 10.10 Mallaig-Glasgow Queen Street.

Britains Least Used Stations

BEASDALE

OPENED	1 APRIL 1901
PRE GROUPING	NORTH BRITISH
MANAGED BY	SCOTRAIL
PLATFORMS	1
REQUEST STOP	YES
SERVICE	MON-FRI SAT SUN
FREQUENCY	C C C

STATION USAGE	NUMBER OF PASSENGERS	LEAST USED
2008/09	200	=15
2009/10	272	21
2010/11	378	32
2011/12	376	=29
2012/13	410	30
2013/14	506	32

Beasdale station is on the Mallaig extension of the West Highland Line 11 miles from Mallaig. It was originally opened as a private station for the nearby Arisaig House and there are very few houses nearby. Beasdale is the least used station on the West Highland Line.

The station building was sold in the 1980s and is now a private holiday home.

On 8 July 2011 156453/45 head towards Mallaig with the 9.07 service from Glasgow Queen Street.

Britains Least Used Stations 199

MORAR

OPENED	1 APRIL 1901
PRE GROUPING	NORTH BRITISH
MANAGED BY	SCOTRAIL
PLATFORMS	1
REQUEST STOP	NO
SERVICE	MON-FRI SAT SUN
FREQUENCY	C C C

STATION USAGE	NUMBER OF PASSENGERS	LEAST USED
2008/09	3216	150
2009/10	3828	159
2010/11	4086	167
2011/12	4826	170
2012/13	4800	169
2013/14	4626	162

Morar station is situated on the West Highland Line three miles from Mallaig. The station serves the village of Morar which is located on the western shores of Loch Morar.

156476 has just seven minutes left of its five hour and twenty minute journey as it calls at Morar with the 12.38 service from Glasgow Queen Street on 25 September 2007.

GARVE

OPENED	19 AUGUST 1870
PRE GROUPING	HIGHLAND RAILWAY
MANAGED BY	SCOTRAIL
PLATFORMS	2
REQUEST STOP	NO
SERVICE	MON-FRI SAT SUN
FREQUENCY	C C D

STATION USAGE	NUMBER OF PASSENGERS	LEAST USED
2008/09	8546	253
2009/10	6898	224
2010/11	5814	198
2011/12	5038	175
2012/13	5384	179
2013/14	5028	176

The Kyle of Lochalsh Line runs from Dingwall nineteen miles from Inverness in a westerly direction to Kyle of Lochalsh a distance of sixty three and a half miles. Garve is the first station on the line twelve miles west of Dingwall. The station serves the village of Garve which is located on the eastern edge of Loch Garve.

All services on the line are in the hands of Scotrail Class 158 DMUs. On 14 July 2014 158723 runs into Garve with the 13.33 Inverness-Kyle of Lochalsh.

Garve is one of three passing places on the line. On 14 July 2014 158716 calls with the 12.05 Kyle of Lochalsh-Inverness.

Britains Least Used Stations

LOCHLUICHART

OPENED	1 AUGUST 1871
PRE GROUPING	HIGHLAND RAILWAY
MANAGED BY	SCOTRAIL
PLATFORMS	1
REQUEST STOP	YES
SERVICE	MON-FRI SAT SUN
FREQUENCY	C C D

STATION USAGE	NUMBER OF PASSENGERS	LEAST USED
2008/09	218	=22
2009/10	392	34
2010/11	324	27
2011/12	442	36
2012/13	400	29
2013/14	612	37

Lochluichart station is situated on the Kyle of Lochalsh Line 17 miles west of Dingwall. The station serves a small settlement on the north bank of Loch Luichart.

The station opened as Lochluichart High and was resited and renamed Lochluichart in 1954.

On weekdays there are four services in each direction. On 8 June 2010 158713 runs into Lochluichart with the 13.34 Inverness- Kyle of Lochalsh.

202   Britains Least Used Stations

ACHANALT

OPENED	19 AUGUST 1870
PRE GROUPING	HIGHLAND RAILWAY
MANAGED BY	SCOTRAIL
PLATFORMS	1
REQUEST STOP	YES
SERVICE	MON-FRI SAT SUN
FREQUENCY	C C D
STATION USAGE	NUMBER OF PASSENGERS	LEAST USED
2008/09	230	24
2009/10	202	14
2010/11	200	=20
2011/12	162	14
2012/13	164	14
2013/14	228	17

Achanalt station is on the Kyle of Lochalsh Line 20 miles west of Dingwall. The station serves a small settlement near Loch Achanalt. With around 200 passengers using the station each year Achanalt is the least used station on the Kyle Line.

158714 is seen entering the station with the 14.35 Kyle of Lochalsh-Inverness on 8 June 2010.

On the same day 47786 passes Achanalt heading towards Kyle of Lochalsh with the luxury Royal Scotsman service.

Britains Least Used Stations

ACHNASHEEN

OPENED	19 AUGUST 1870
PRE GROUPING	HIGHLAND RAILWAY
MANAGED BY	SCOTRAIL
PLATFORMS	2
REQUEST STOP	NO
SERVICE	MON-FRI SAT SUN
FREQUENCY	C C D

STATION USAGE	NUMBER OF PASSENGERS	LEAST USED
2008/09	3202	149
2009/10	3614	150
2010/11	3698	155
2011/12	3998	151
2012/13	3566	144
2013/14	3972	145

Achnasheen station is on the Kyle of Lochalsh Line 28 miles west of Dingwall. The station serves the small village of Achnasheen. The station building serves as a postal distribution point.

Achnasheen is the second passing point on the line. 158701 arrives with the 14.37 Kyle of Lochalsh-Inverness on 14 July 2014.

On the same date 158723 heads for Kyle of Lochalsh with the 13.33 service from Inverness.

204   Britains Least Used Stations

ACHNASHELLACH

OPENED	19 AUGUST 1870
PRE GROUPING	HIGHLAND RAILWAY
MANAGED BY	SCOTRAIL
PLATFORMS	1
REQUEST STOP	YES
SERVICE	MON-FRI SAT SUN
FREQUENCY	C C D

STATION USAGE	NUMBER OF PASSENGERS	LEAST USED
2008/09	646	47
2009/10	778	54
2010/11	738	50
2011/12	1084	59
2012/13	1054	=59
2013/14	976	53

Achnashellach station is situated on the Kyle of Lochalsh Line 40 miles west of Dingwall and 23 miles from Kyle. The station serves a small settlement located to the north of Loch Dughaill.

158704 enters Achnashellach with the 12.03 Kyle of Lochalsh -Inverness on 8 June 2010.

On the same date 158714 calls with the 11.01 Inverness- Kyle of Lochalsh.

Britains Least Used Stations 205

ATTADALE

OPENED	JULY 1880
PRE GROUPING	HIGHLAND RAILWAY
MANAGED BY	SCOTRAIL
PLATFORMS	1
REQUEST STOP	YES
SERVICE	MON-FRI SAT SUN
FREQUENCY	C C D

STATION USAGE	NUMBER OF PASSENGERS	LEAST USED
2008/09	472	33
2009/10	478	38
2010/11	526	40
2011/12	968	55
2012/13	658	42
2013/14	998	54

Attadale station is on the Kyle of Lochalsh Line two and a half miles west of Strathcarron and 15 miles from Kyle. The station serves the small village of Attadale which is situated on the southern shore of Loch Carron in one of the most picturesque locations of the line.

With Loch Carron in the background 158712 approaches Attadale with the 10.52 Inverness-Kyle of Lochalsh on 17 June 2008.

On the same date 158705 runs into the station with the 12.00 Kyle of Lochalsh-Inverness.

Britains Least Used Stations

STROMEFERRY

OPENED	19 AUGUST 1870
PRE GROUPING	HIGHLAND RAILWAY
MANAGED BY	SCOTRAIL
PLATFORMS	1
REQUEST STOP	NO
SERVICE	MON-FRI SAT SUN
FREQUENCY	C C D

STATION USAGE	NUMBER OF PASSENGERS	LEAST USED
2008/09	1000	62
2009/10	1064	=63
2010/11	1438	73
2011/12	2218	109
2012/13	2074	98
2013/14	1874	89

Stromeferry station is on the Kyle of Lochalsh Line ten miles from Kyle. The station serves the village of Stromeferry situated on the south shore of Loch Carron. When the line opened in 1870 Stromeferry was the terminus of the line and it remained so until 1897 when the line was extended to Kyle of Lochalsh.

Taken from the bridge at the west of the station, 158712 is seen with the 10.52 Inverness-Kyle of Lochalsh on 17 June 2008.

Later the same day 158724 enters Stromeferry with the 12.41 Inverness- Kyle of Lochalsh.

Britains Least Used Stations

DUNCRAIG

OPENED	2 NOVEMBER 1897
PRE GROUPING	HIGHLAND RAILWAY
MANAGED BY	SCOTRAIL
PLATFORMS	1
REQUEST STOP	YES
SERVICE	MON-FRI SAT SUN
FREQUENCY	C C D

STATION USAGE	NUMBER OF PASSENGERS	LEAST USED
2008/09	388	=30
2009/10	394	35
2010/11	602	43
2011/12	722	=46
2012/13	784	47
2013/14	534	34

Duncraig station is situated on the Kyle of Lochalsh Line six and a half miles from Kyle. When the station first opened in 1897 it was known as Duncraig Platform and was a private station serving the nearby Duncraig Castle. It was first opened to the public in 1949. The station closed in 1964 and reopened in 1976.

The station features a hexagonal building used as a waiting room seen here in this delightful view with Loch Carron in the background.

158712 is seen entering Duncraig with the 15.13 Kyle of Lochalsh- Inverness on 17 June 2008.

208   Britains Least Used Stations

DUIRINISH

OPENED	2 NOVEMBER 1897
PRE GROUPING	HIGHLAND RAILWAY
MANAGED BY	SCOTRAIL
PLATFORMS	1
REQUEST STOP	YES
SERVICE	MON-FRI SAT SUN
FREQUENCY	C C D

STATION USAGE	NUMBER OF PASSENGERS	LEAST USED
2008/09	742	52
2009/10	620	47
2010/11	808	51
2011/12	702	45
2012/13	804	49
2013/14	970	52

Duirinish is the final station on the Kyle of Lochalsh Line just under four miles from Kyle. The small village of Duirinish is located half a mile to the east of the station.

158705 is first seen entering Duirinish and then waiting to leave with the 12.00 Kyle of Lochalsh -Inverness on 17 June 2008.

Britains Least Used Stations 209

FEARN

OPENED	1ST JUNE 1864
PRE GROUPING	HIGHLAND RAILWAY
MANAGED BY	SCOTRAIL
PLATFORMS	1
REQUEST STOP	NO
SERVICE	MON-FRI SAT SUN
FREQUENCY	B B C

STATION USAGE	NUMBER OF PASSENGERS	LEAST USED
2008/09	7724	238
2009/10	6790	222
2010/11	6720	209
2011/12	7818	224
2012/13	7226	210
2013/14	6606	194

The Far North Line runs from Inverness to Wick a distance of 175 miles. The line to Kyle of Lochalsh divides at Dingwall. Fearn station is situated 41 miles from Inverness and 22 miles from Dingwall. The station serves the village of Hill of Fearn and several other small villages to the east of the station.

There are four services in each direction between Inverness and Wick Monday to Saturday with one each way on Sunday. 158711 is seen arriving with the 8.12 Wick-Inverness on 12 July 2011.

In addition to the four Inverness-Wick services Fearn receives four additional peak hour services from Inverness. On 14 July 2014 158703 calls with the 17.13 Inverness-Ardgay.

Britains Least Used Stations

CULRAIN

OPENED	1 JULY 1870
PRE GROUPING	HIGHLAND RAILWAY
MANAGED BY	SCOTRAIL
PLATFORMS	1
REQUEST STOP	YES
SERVICE	MON-FRI SAT SUN
FREQUENCY	C C D

STATION USAGE	NUMBER OF PASSENGERS	LEAST USED
2008/09	1886	109
2009/10	1722	93
2010/11	1708	90
2011/12	526	39
2012/13	474	34
2013/14	628	39

Culrain station is on the Far North Line 61 miles from Inverness. The station serves the small village of Culrain which is situated on the west bank of the Kyle of Sutherland.

Culrain station lies close to Carbisdale Castle which was used as a youth hostel until 2011. Since its closure passenger numbers have decreased from over 1700 to around 500. On 18 July 2006 a number of students staying at the hostel are seen boarding the train to Inverness. 158704 is employed on the 16.05 service from Wick.

Britains Least Used Stations

INVERSHIN

OPENED	13 APRIL 1868
PRE GROUPING	HIGHLAND RAILWAY
MANAGED BY	SCOTRAIL
PLATFORMS	1
REQUEST STOP	YES
SERVICE	MON-FRI SAT SUN
FREQUENCY	C C D

STATION USAGE	NUMBER OF PASSENGERS	LEAST USED
2008/09	220	23
2009/10	282	24
2010/11	512	39
2011/12	386	=31
2012/13	690	44
2013/14	790	43

Invershin station is on the Far North Line and is located half a mile from Culrain on the opposite side of the Kyle of Sutherland. There are very few houses nearby.

The two stations are connected by a footbridge alongside the railway which crosses the Kyle of Sutherland at its narrowest point.

158716 is seen departing Invershin with the 12.36 Wick - Inverness on 14 July 2011.

Britains Least Used Stations

LAIRG

OPENED	13 APRIL 1868
PRE GROUPING	HIGHLAND RAILWAY
MANAGED BY	SCOTRAIL
PLATFORMS	2 (STAGGERED)
REQUEST STOP	NO
SERVICE	MON-FRI SAT SUN
FREQUENCY	C C D

STATION USAGE	NUMBER OF PASSENGERS	LEAST USED
2008/09	5280	195
2009/10	5542	195
2010/11	6098	200
2011/12	6330	198
2012/13	6176	194
2013/14	7440	211

Lairg station is on the Far North Line 67 miles from Inverness. The station is situated one mile south of the village of Lairg which lies on the southern banks of Loch Shin.

Taken from the footbridge 158724 arrives at Lairg with the 14.00 Inverness-Wick on 15 July 2014. The former station building and original southbound platform can be seen on the left of the picture.

Scotrail Class 158 DMUs cover all services on the Far North Line. 158707 stands in the resited platform with the 12.35 Wick-Inverness on 15 July 2014.

Britains Least Used Stations   213

ROGART

OPENED	13 APRIL 1868
PRE GROUPING	HIGHLAND RAILWAY
MANAGED BY	SCOTRAIL
PLATFORMS	2
REQUEST STOP	YES
SERVICE	MON-FRI SAT SUN
FREQUENCY	C C D

STATION USAGE	NUMBER OF PASSENGERS	LEAST USED
2008/09	1538	96
2009/10	1844	103
2010/11	1456	74
2011/12	1736	87
2012/13	1662	81
2013/14	1662	=80

Rogart station is on the Far North Line 77 miles from Inverness. The station serves the village of Rogart which is situated on the A839 road between Lairg and Golspie. The station closed in June 1960 along with six other stations on the line. Whilst the other stations remain closed Rogart reopened in March 1961.

The station buildings have been converted into private residential use. The station yard contains lots of old railway memorabilia and three Mark 2 coaches which have been converted to provide bunkhouse accommodation.

158710 calls at Rogart with the 12.36 Wick-Inverness on 13 July 2011. The Mark 2 coaches can be seen on the left of the picture.

Britains Least Used Stations

DUNROBIN CASTLE

OPENED	1 NOVEMBER 1870
PRE GROUPING	HIGHLAND RAILWAY
MANAGED BY	SCOTRAIL
PLATFORMS	1
REQUEST STOP	YES
SERVICE	MON-FRI SAT SUN
FREQUENCY	C C D
	(NO WINTER SERVICE)
STATION	NUMBER OF LEAST
USAGE	PASSENGERS USED
2008/09	572 44
2009/10	488 39
2010/11	594 42
2011/12	628 42
2012/13	628 40
2013/14	916 49

Dunrobin Castle station is on the Far North Line 87 miles from Inverness and two and a half miles north of Golspie. It was originally opened as a private station for the Castle home of the Duke of Sutherland before being opened to the public.

The building used as a waiting room dates from 1902 and is a category B listed building.

The station was closed between January 1965 and June 1985, and is now only open during the summer. 158701 is seen departing with the 13.59 Inverness-Wick on 13 July 2011.

Britains Least Used Stations   215

BRORA

OPENED	1 NOVEMBER 1870
PRE GROUPING	HIGHLAND RAILWAY
MANAGED BY	SCOTRAIL
PLATFORMS	2
REQUEST STOP	NO
SERVICE FREQUENCY	MON-FRI SAT SUN C C D

STATION USAGE	NUMBER OF PASSENGERS	LEAST USED
2008/09	4660	184
2009/10	5614	198
2010/11	5780	197
2011/12	5164	177
2012/13	5556	185
2013/14	6380	192

Brora station is situated on the Far North Line 90 miles from Inverness. The station serves the small town of Brora. With a population of over 1,000 it is one of the largest communities served by the line.

On 15 July 2014 158707 is seen running into Brora with the 7.04 Inverness-Wick.

On the same morning 158715 calls with the 6.20 Wick- Inverness.

Britains Least Used Stations

HELMSDALE

OPENED	16 MAY 1871
PRE GROUPING	HIGHLAND RAILWAY
MANAGED BY	SCOTRAIL
PLATFORMS	2
REQUEST STOP	NO
SERVICE	MON-FRI SAT SUN
FREQUENCY	C C D

STATION USAGE	NUMBER OF PASSENGERS	LEAST USED
2008/09	5646	202
2009/10	5680	=199
2010/11	5656	196
2011/12	6086	193
2012/13	5828	192
2013/14	5778	186

Helmsdale station is situated on the Far North Line 101 miles from Inverness. The station serves the village of Helmsdale a small fishing port on the North Sea. The station building has recently been restored and converted for use as holiday accommodation.

On 14 July 2014 in fading light 158715 calls at Helmsdale with the 17.54 Inverness-Wick.

The following morning 158715 is seen again with the 6.20 Wick-Inverness.

Britains Least Used Stations 217

KILDONAN

OPENED	28 JULY 1874
PRE GROUPING	HIGHLAND RAILWAY
MANAGED BY	SCOTRAIL
PLATFORMS	1
REQUEST STOP	YES
SERVICE	MON-FRI SAT SUN
FREQUENCY	C C D

STATION USAGE	NUMBER OF PASSENGERS	LEAST USED
2008/09	174	13
2009/10	204	=15
2010/11	142	15
2011/12	240	22
2012/13	62	5
2013/14	144	13

Kildonan station is situated on the Far North Line 111 miles from Inverness. There are very few houses nearby and it is one of the least used stations on the rail network.

158724 calls with the 14.00 Inverness-Wick on 15 July 2014. Because of the low platform, steps are provided to assist passengers board and alight from trains.

On the same date 158701 arrives at Kildonan with the 16.00 Wick-Inverness.

KINBRACE

OPENED	28 JULY 1874
PRE GROUPING	HIGHLAND RAILWAY
MANAGED BY	SCOTRAIL
PLATFORMS	1
REQUEST STOP	YES
SERVICE FREQUENCY	MON-FRI SAT SUN C C D

STATION USAGE	NUMBER OF PASSENGERS	LEAST USED
2008/09	792	54
2009/10	410	36
2010/11	448	35
2011/12	778	49
2012/13	1090	62
2013/14	1092	55

Kinbrace station is on the Far North Line 118 miles from Inverness. There is very little settlement near the station but passenger numbers have shown a marked increase over the past few years. The station building is now a private residence.

158710 runs into the station with the 12.36 Wick-Inverness on 13 July 2011.

Britains Least Used Stations

219

FORSINARD

OPENED	28 JULY 1874
PRE GROUPING	HIGHLAND RAILWAY
MANAGED BY	SCOTRAIL
PLATFORMS	2
REQUEST STOP	NO
SERVICE	MON-FRI SAT SUN
FREQUENCY	C C D

STATION USAGE	NUMBER OF PASSENGERS	LEAST USED
2008/09	1836	106
2009/10	1496	80
2010/11	1770	91
2011/12	1970	97
2012/13	2088	99
2013/14	1718	83

Forsinard station is on the Far North Line 126 miles from Inverness. The station serves the small village of Forsinard which is located in an area where the Royal Society for the Protection of Birds runs a 25,000 acre Nature Reserve. The station building is used as the RSPB Visitor Centre.

Forsinard is the first passing place south of Wick. On 14 July 2011 158716 calls with the 12.36 Wick-Inverness, while 158702 can be seen heading for Wick with the 10.38 service from Inverness.

158710 pauses at Forsinard with the 17.54 Inverness-Wick on 13 July 2011.

ALTNABREAC

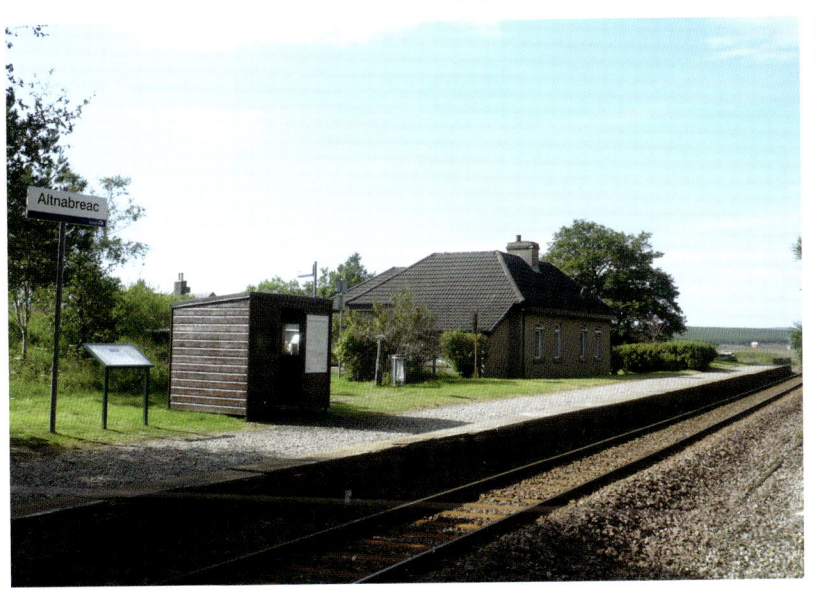

OPENED	28 JULY 1874
PRE GROUPING	HIGHLAND RAILWAY
MANAGED BY	SCOTRAIL
PLATFORMS	1
REQUEST STOP	YES
SERVICE	MON-FRI SAT SUN
FREQUENCY	C C D
STATION	NUMBER OF LEAST
USAGE	PASSENGERS USED
2008/09	212 18
2009/10	156 8
2010/11	172 17
2011/12	238 21
2012/13	296 26
2013/14	138 12

Altnabreac station is on the Far North Line 134 miles from Inverness. It is one of the remotest stations on the rail network with just a couple of houses situated nearby. It can only be approached on an unsurfaced road of twenty miles unsuitable for most vehicles.

158710 calls at the remote location with the 6.20 Wick-Inverness service on 14 July 2011.

Later the same morning 158716 arrives with the 7.06 Inverness-Wick.

Britains Least Used Stations

SCOTSCALDER

OPENED	28 JULY 1874
PRE GROUPING	HIGHLAND RAILWAY
MANAGED BY	SCOTRAIL
PLATFORMS	1
REQUEST STOP	YES
SERVICE	MON-FRI SAT SUN
FREQUENCY	C C D

STATION USAGE	NUMBER OF PASSENGERS	LEAST USED
2008/09	256	25
2009/10	184	12
2010/11	246	23
2011/12	214	20
2012/13	460	=32
2013/14	376	28

Scotscalder station is situated on the Far North Line 143 miles from Inverness. The station serves several small settlements in the area. In 1988 the station building was sold and converted into residential dwelling. For a time it was available to rent as a holiday home but is now back as a private residence.

158716 calls with the 7.06 Inverness -Wick on 14 July 2011.

Later that day the same unit is seen returning to Inverness with the 12.36 service from Wick.

Britains Least Used Stations

GEORGEMAS JUNCTION

OPENED	28 JULY 1874
PRE GROUPING	HIGHLAND RAILWAY
MANAGED BY	SCOTRAIL
PLATFORMS	1
REQUEST STOP	NO
SERVICE	MON-FRI SAT SUN
FREQUENCY	C C D

STATION USAGE	NUMBER OF PASSENGERS	LEAST USED
2008/09	1500	92
2009/10	1482	79
2010/11	1630	84
2011/12	1682	86
2012/13	1906	92
2013/14	1652	78

Georgemas Junction station is situated on the Far North Line 147 miles from Inverness. The station serves the village of Halkirk over one mile away and several other small settlements. It is the most northerly junction on the rail network, the line dividing with one line to Thurso and one to Wick.

On arrival trains reverse to make the seven mile trip to Thurso. The train then returns to Georgemas Junction and continues to the terminus at Wick. The line straight ahead is from Inverness while the line to Thurso can be seen branching off to the right.

On 15 July 2014 158707 has arrived with the 7.04 from Inverness. It will now reverse to make the trip to Thurso.

Britains Least Used Stations

GEORGEMAS JUNCTION

158707 has arrived back from Thurso and is about to make the fourteen mile journey to Wick.(above)

After a one hour stay at Wick 158707 returns to Georgemas Junction with the 12.35 to Inverness. The train will once more make the round trip to Thurso before continuing its journey to Inverness.(left)

With the footbridge visible 158710 has arrived with the 6.20 Wick-Inverness on 14 July 2011.(below left)

158704 calls with the 10.29 Inverness-Wick on 18 July 2006. The second platform and footbridge were removed in 2012 to make way for a freight terminal for Direct Rail Services. (below)

ATTADALE Kyle of Lochalsh Line 17-6-08

ST COLUMB ROAD Newquay branch 4-6-10

BERNEY ARMS Between Norwich and Great Yarmouth 31-7-11

Britains Least Used Stations

NORTHERN ENGLAND

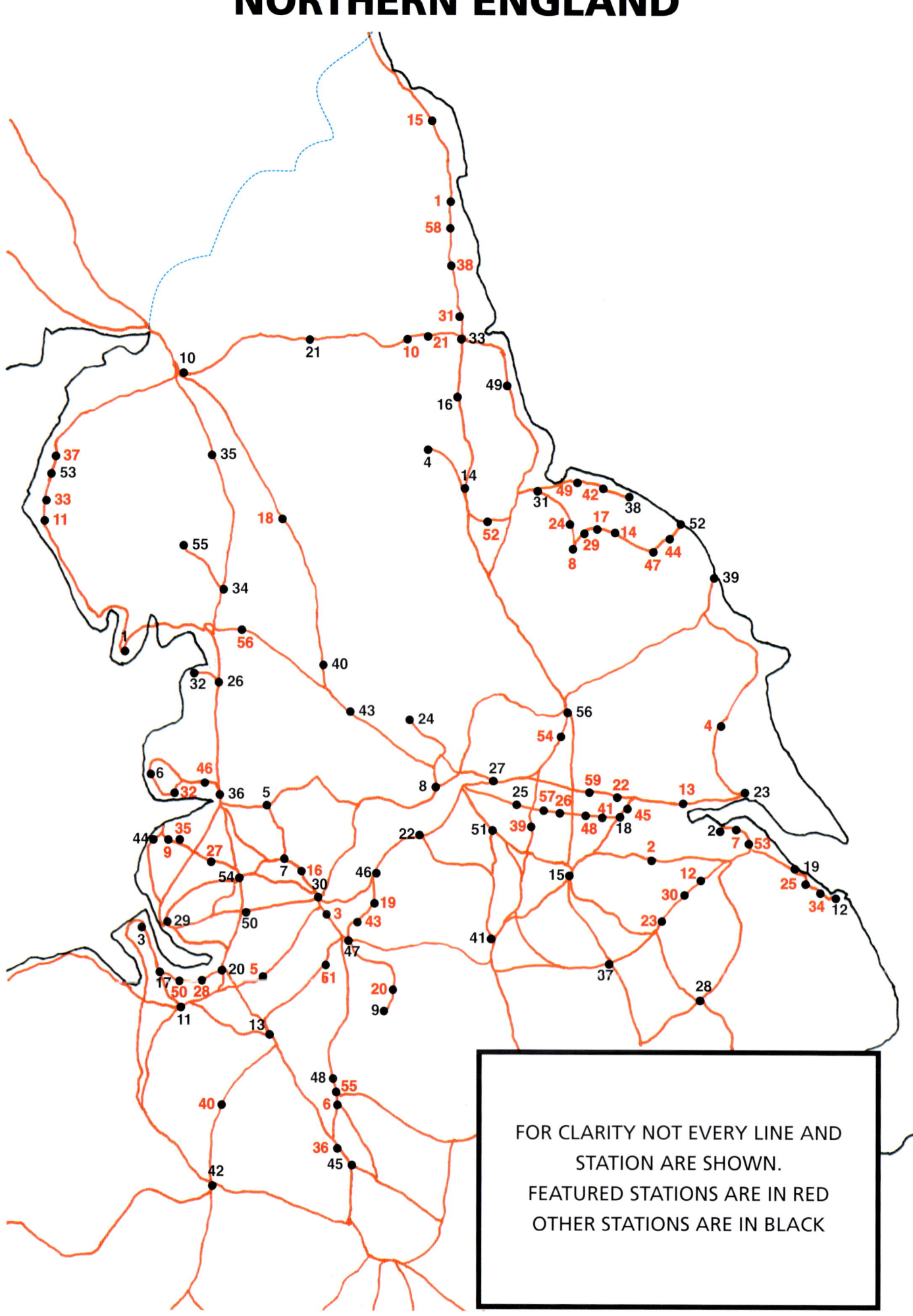

FOR CLARITY NOT EVERY LINE AND STATION ARE SHOWN.
FEATURED STATIONS ARE IN RED
OTHER STATIONS ARE IN BLACK

1	ACKLINGTON		1	BARROW
2	ALTHORPE		2	BARTON-ON-HUMBER
3	ARDWICK		3	BIRKENHEAD
4	ARRAM		4	BISHOP AUCKLAND
5	ASHLEY		5	BLACKBURN
6	BARLASTON		6	BLACKPOOL
7	BARROW HAVEN		7	BOLTON
8	BATTERSBY		8	BRADFORD
9	BESCAR LANE		9	BUXTON
10	BLAYDON		10	CARLISLE
11	BRAYSTONES		11	CHESTER
12	BRIGG		12	CLEETHORPES
13	BROOMFLEET		13	CREWE
14	CASTLETON MOOR		14	DARLINGTON
15	CHATHILL		15	DONCASTER
16	CLIFTON		16	DURHAM
17	COMMONDALE		17	ELLESMERE PORT
18	DENT		18	GOOLE
19	DENTON		19	GRIMSBY TOWN
20	DOVE HOLES		20	HELSBY
21	DUNSTON		21	HEXHAM
22	EASTRINGTON		22	HUDDERSFIELD
23	GAINSBOROUGH CENTRAL		23	HULL
24	GREAT AYTON		24	ILKLEY
25	GRIMSBY DOCKS		25	KNOTTINGLEY
26	HENSALL		26	LANCASTER
27	HOSCAR		27	LEEDS
28	INCE & ELTON		28	LINCOLN
29	KILDALE		29	LIVERPOOL
30	KIRTON LINDSEY		30	MANCHESTER
31	MANORS		31	MIDDLESBROUGH
32	MOSS SIDE		32	MORECAMBE
33	NETHERTOWN		33	NEWCASTLE
34	NEW CLEE		34	OXENHOLME
35	NEW LANE		35	PENRITH
36	NORTON BRIDGE		36	PRESTON
37	PARTON		37	RETFORD
38	PEGSWOOD		38	SALTBURN
39	PONTEFRACT BAGHILL		39	SCARBOROUGH
40	PREES		40	SETTLE
41	RAWCLIFFE		41	SHEFFIELD
42	REDCAR BRITISH STEEL		42	SHREWSBURY
43	REDDISH SOUTH		43	SKIPTON
44	RUSWARP		44	SOUTHPORT
45	SALTMARSHE		45	STAFFORD
46	SALWICK		46	STALYBRIDGE
47	SLEIGHTS		47	STOCKPORT
48	SNAITH		48	STOKE ON TRENT
49	SOUTH BANK		49	SUNDERLAND
50	STANLOW & THORNTON		50	WARRINGTON
51	STYAL		51	WAKEFIELD
52	TEESSIDE AIRPORT		52	WHITBY
53	THORNTON ABBEY		53	WHITEHAVEN
54	ULLESKELF		54	WIGAN
55	WEDGWOOD		55	WINDERMERE
56	WENNINGTON		56	YORK
57	WHITLEY BRIDGE			
58	WIDDRINGTON			
59	WRESSLE			

Britains Least Used Stations

SOUTH EAST & EAST MIDLANDS

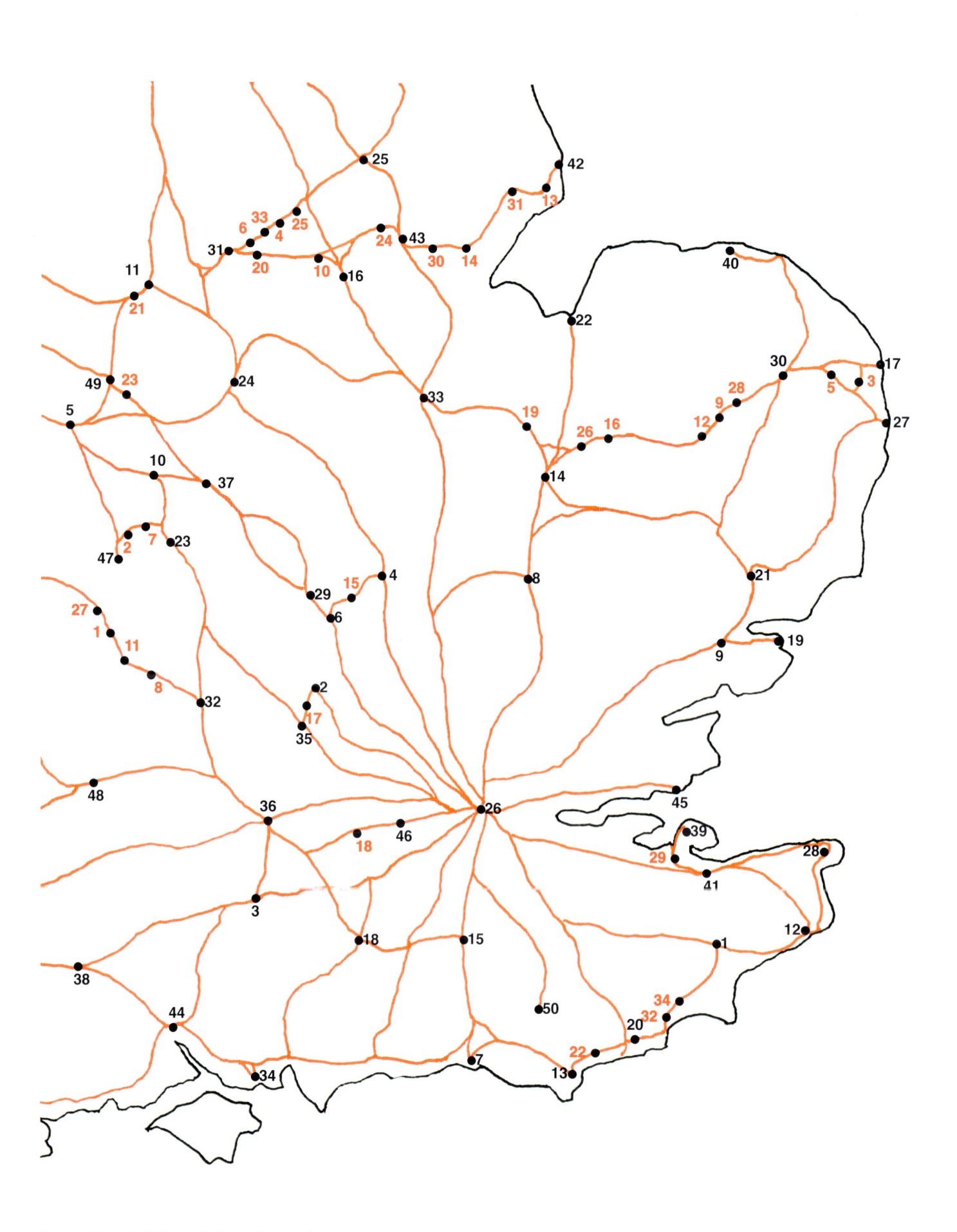

1	ASCOTT-UNDER-WYCHWOOD		1	ASHFORD
2	BEARLEY		2	AYLESBURY
3	BERNEY ARMS		3	BASINGSTOKE
4	BLEASBY		4	BEDFORD
5	BUCKENHAM		5	BIRMINGHAM
6	BURTON JOYCE		6	BLETCHLEY
7	CLAVERDON		7	BRIGHTON
8	COMBE		8	CAMBRIDGE
9	ECCLES ROAD		9	COLCHESTER
10	ELTON & ORSTON		10	COVENTRY
11	FINSTOCK		11	DERBY
12	HARLING ROAD		12	DOVER
13	HAVENHOUSE		13	EASTBOURNE
14	HUBBERTS BRIDGE		14	ELY
15	KEMPSTON HARDWICK		15	GATWICK AIRPORT
16	LAKENHEATH		16	GRANTHAM
17	LITTLE KIMBLE		17	GREAT YARMOUTH
18	LONGCROSS		18	GUILDFORD
19	MANEA		19	HARWICH
20	NETHERFIELD		20	HASTINGS
21	PEARTREE		21	IPSWICH
22	PEVENSEY BAY		22	KINGS LYNN
23	POLESWORTH		23	LEAMINGTON SPA
24	RAUCEBY		24	LEICESTER
25	ROLLESTON		25	LINCOLN
26	SHIPPEA HILL		26	LONDON
27	SHIPTON		27	LOWESTOFT
28	SPOONER ROW		28	MARGATE
29	SWALE		29	MILTON KEYNES
30	SWINESHEAD		30	NORWICH
31	THORPE CULVERT		31	NOTTINGHAM
32	THREE OAKS		32	OXFORD
33	THURGARTON		33	PETERBOROUGH
34	WINCHELSEA		34	PORTSMOUTH
			35	PRINCES RISBOROUGH
			36	READING
			37	RUGBY
			38	SALISBURY
			39	SHEERNESS-ON-SEA
			40	SHERINGHAM
			41	SITTINGBOURNE
			42	SKEGNESS
			43	SLEAFORD
			44	SOUTHAMPTON
			45	SOUTHEND
			46	STAINS
			47	STRATFORD-UPON-AVON
			48	SWINDON
			49	TAMWORTH
			50	UCKFIELD

Britains Least Used Stations

WALES & SOUTH WEST

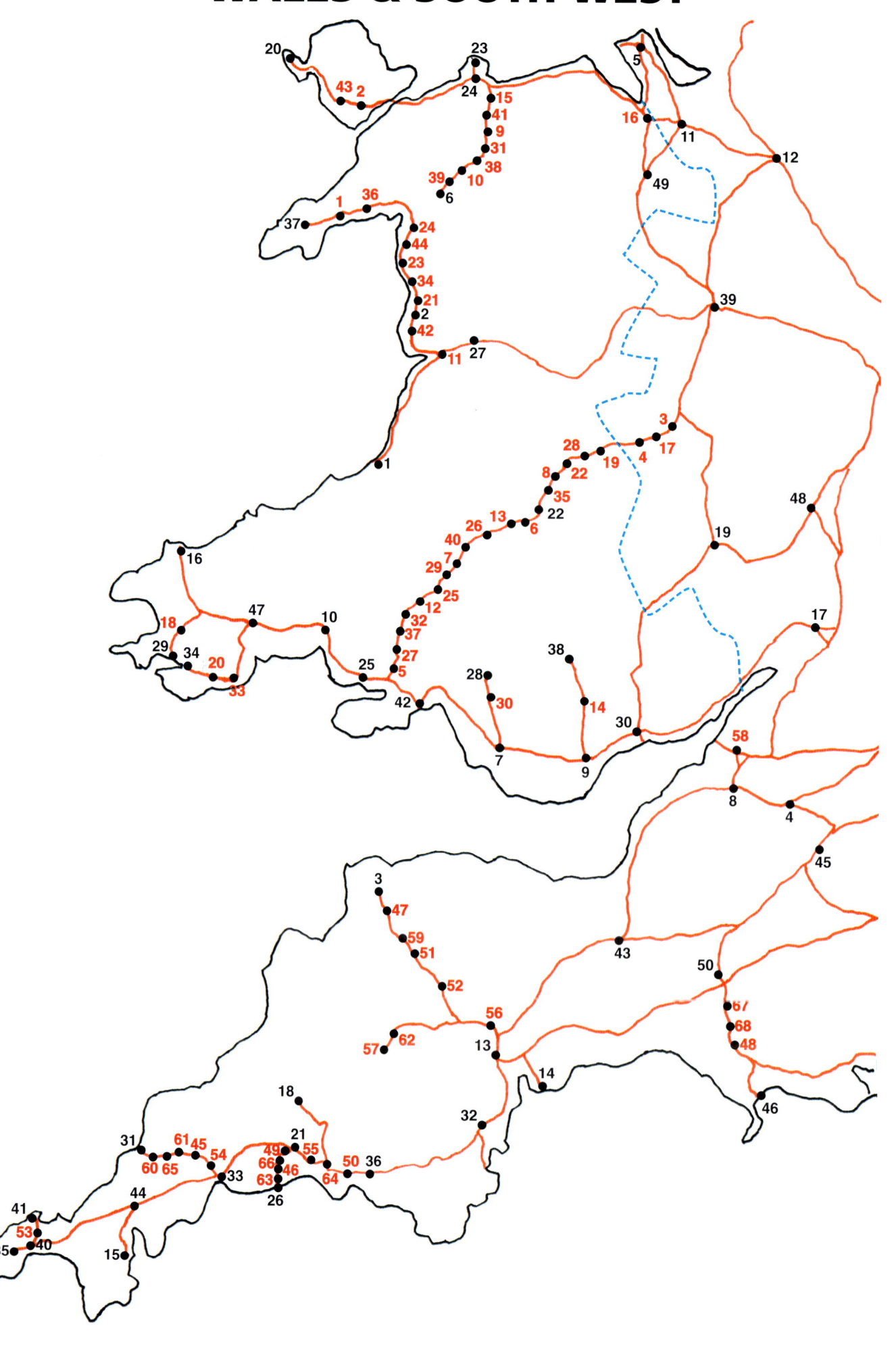

Britains Least Used Stations

1	ABERERCH		1	ABERYSTWYTH
2	BODORGAN		2	BARMOUTH
3	BROOME		3	BARNSTAPLE
4	BUCKNELL		4	BATH
5	BYNEA		5	BIDSTON
6	CILMERI		6	BLAENAU FFESTINIOG
7	CYNGHORDY		7	BRIDGEND
8	DOLAU		8	BRISTOL TEMPLE MEADS
9	DOLGARROG		9	CARDIFF
10	DOLWYDDELAN		10	CARMARTHEN
11	DOVEY JUNCTION		11	CHESTER
12	FFAIRFACH		12	CREWE
13	GARTH (POWYS)		13	EXETER ST DAVIDS
14	GILFACH FARGOED		14	EXMOUTH
15	GLAN CONWY		15	FALMOUTH
16	HAWARDEN BRIDGE		16	FISHGUARD HARBOUR
17	HOPTON HEATH		17	GLOUCESTER
18	JOHNSTON		18	GUNNISLAKE
19	KNUCKLAS		19	HEREFORD
20	LAMPHEY		20	HOLYHEAD
21	LLANABER		21	LISKEARD
22	LLANBISTER ROAD		22	LLANDRINDOD WELLS
23	LLANDANWG		23	LLANDUDNO
24	LLANDECWYN		24	LLANDUDNO JUNCTION
25	LLANGADOG		25	LLANELLI
26	LLANGAMMARCH		26	LOOE
27	LLANGENNECH		27	MACHYNLLETH
28	LLANGYNLLO		28	MAESTEG
29	LLANWRDA		29	MILFORD HAVEN
30	MAESTEG EWENNY ROAD		30	NEWPORT
31	NORTH LLANRWST		31	NEWQUAY
32	PANTYFFYNNON		32	NEWTON ABBOT
33	PENALLY		33	PAR
34	PENSARN		34	PEMBROKE DOCK
35	PEN-Y-BONT		35	PENZANCE
36	PENYCHAIN		36	PLYMOUTH
37	PONTARDDULAIS		37	PWLLHELI
38	PONT-Y-PANT		38	RHYMNEY
39	ROMAN BRIDGE		39	SHREWSBURY
40	SUGAR LOAF		40	ST ERTH
41	TAL-Y-CAFN		41	ST IVES
42	TONFANAU		42	SWANSEA
43	TY CROES		43	TAUNTON
44	TYGWYN		44	TRURO
45	BUGLE		45	WESTBURY
46	CAUSELAND		46	WEYMOUTH
47	CHAPELTON		47	WHITLAND
48	CHETNOLE		48	WORCESTER
49	COOMBE JUNCTION HALT		49	WREXHAM
50	KEYHAM		50	YEOVIL PEN MILL
51	KINGS NYMPTON			
52	LAPFORD			
53	LELANT			
54	LUXULYAN			
55	MENHENIOT			
56	NEWTON ST CYRES			
57	OKEHAMPTON			
58	PILNING			
59	PORTSMOUTH ARMS			
60	QUINTREL DOWNS			
61	ROCHE			
62	SAMPFORD COURTENAY			
63	SANDPLACE			
64	ST BUDEAUX FERRY ROAD			
65	ST COLUMB ROAD			
66	ST KEYNE WISHING WELL HALT			
67	THORNFORD			
68	YETMINSTER			

SCOTLAND

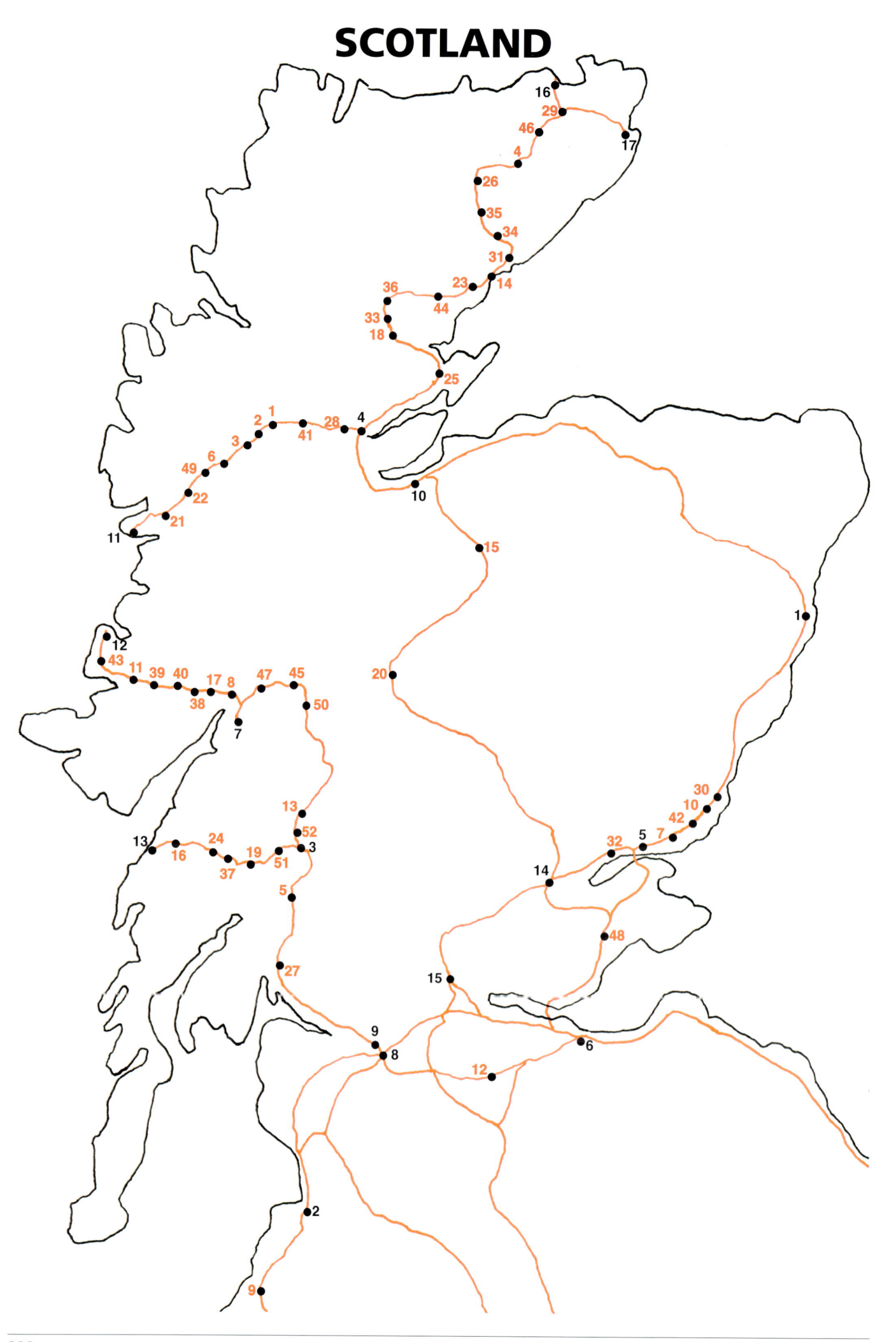

1	ACHANALT		1	ABERDEEN
2	ACHNASHEEN		2	AYR
3	ACHNASHELLACH		3	CRIANLARICH
4	ALTNABREAC		4	DINGWALL
5	ARDLUI		5	DUNDEE
6	ATTADALE		6	EDINBURGH WAVERLEY
7	BALMOSSIE		7	FORT WILLIAM
8	BANAVIE		8	GLASGOW CENTRAL
9	BARRHILL		9	GLASGOW QUEEN STREET
10	BARRY LINKS		10	INVERNESS
11	BEASDALE		11	KYLE OF LOCHALSH
12	BREICH		12	MALLAIG
13	BRIDGE OF ORCHY		13	OBAN
14	BRORA		14	PERTH
15	CARRBRIDGE		15	STIRLING
16	CONNEL FERRY		16	THURSO
17	CORPACH		17	WICK
18	CULRAIN			
19	DALMALLY			
20	DALWHINNIE			
21	DUIRINISH			
22	DUNCRAIG			
23	DUNROBIN CASTLE			
24	FALLS OF CRUACHAN			
25	FEARN			
26	FORSINARD			
27	GARELOCHHEAD			
28	GARVE			
29	GEORGEMAS JUNCTION			
30	GOLF STREET			
31	HELMSDALE			
32	INVERGOWRIE			
33	INVERSHIN			
34	KILDONAN			
35	KINBRACE			
36	LAIRG			
37	LOCH AWE			
38	LOCH EIL OUTWARD BOUND			
39	LOCHAILORT			
40	LOCHEILSIDE			
41	LOCHLUICHART			
42	MONIFIETH			
43	MORAR			
44	ROGART			
45	ROY BRIDGE			
46	SCOTSCALDER			
47	SPEAN BRIDGE			
48	SPRINGFIELD			
49	STROMEFERRY			
50	TULLOCH			
51	TYNDRUM LOWER			
52	UPPER TYNDRUM			

Britains Least Used Stations

LEAST USED STATIONS 2013/14

1 TEESSIDE AIRPORT	8	
2 SHIPPEA HILL	12	
3 REDDISH SOUTH	26	
4 BARRY LINKS	40	
5 COOMBE JUNCTION HALT	48	
6 BREICH	64	
7 BUCKENHAM	80	
8 PILNING	88	
9 GOLF STREET	90	
10 DENTON	110	
11 KIRTON LINDSEY	120	
12 ALTNABRAEC	138	
13 KILDONAN	144	
14 SAMPFORD COURTENAY	146	
15 ELTON & ORSTON	166	
16 ACKLINGTON	176	
17 ACHANALT	228	
18 CHAPELTON	232	
19 SUGAR LOAF	240	
20 HENSALL	276	
21 HAVENHOUSE	278	
22 CLIFTON	298	
=23 RAWCLIFFE	314	
=23 STANLOW & THORNTON	314	
25 HUBBERTS BRIDGE	334	
26 THORPE CULVERT	340	
27 NEW CLEE	348	
28 SCOTSCALDER	376	
29 LAKENHEATH	378	
30 SPOONER ROW	388	
31 FALLS OF CRUACHAN	498	
32 BEASDALE	506	
33 LOCH EIL OUTWARD B.	522	
34 DUNCRAIG	534	
35 ARDWICK	568	
36 LOCHEILSIDE	588	
37 LOCHLUICHART	612	
38 BRAYSTONES	620	
39 CULRAIN	628	
40 SPRINGFIELD	680	
41 POLESWORTH	702	
42 ROMAN BRIDGE	764	
43 INVERSHIN	790	
44 LLANGYNLLO	806	
45 DOLGARROG	828	
46 PORTSMOUTH ARMS	844	
47 WHITLEY BRIDGE	864	
48 LLANDECWYN	880	
49 DUNROBIN CASTLE	916	
50 BRIGG	922	
51 INCE & ELTON	944	
52 DUIRINISH	970	
53 ACHNASHELLACH	976	
54 ATTADALE	998	
55 KINBRACE	1092	
56 NETHERTOWN	1160	
57 PEGSWOOD	1166	
=58 BEARLEY	1220	
=58 GAINSBOROUGH CENTRAL	1220	
60 QUINTREL DOWNS	1286	
61 THORNTON ABBEY	1298	
62 CYNGHORDY	1312	
63 GARTH (POWYS)	1322	
64 BROOMFLEET	1326	
65 ST KEYNE WISHING WELL	1362	
66 TYGWYN	1364	
67 ABERERCH	1380	
68 LLANBISTER ROAD	1390	
69 DOLAU	1406	
70 REDCAR BRITISH STEEL	1418	
71 PONT-Y-PANT	1424	
72 HOSCAR	1446	
73 BALMOSSIE	1446	
74 BERNEY ARMS	1510	
=75 PEN-Y-BONT	1548	
=75 WRESSLE	1548	
77 BATTERSBY	1592	
78 GEORGEMAS JUNCTION	1652	
79 LUXULYAN	1654	
=80 BYNEA	1662	
=80 ROGART	1662	
82 COMBE	1684	
83 FORSINARD	1718	
84 EASTRINGTON	1738	
85 SNAITH	1776	
86 PENSARN	1810	
87 DOVEY JUNCTION	1828	
88 SANDPLACE	1860	
89 STROMEFERRY	1874	
90 RAUCEBY	1898	
91 ARRAM	1900	
92 FINSTOCK	1920	
93 ROCHE	1950	
94 KILDALE	1960	
95 THURGARTON	1972	
96 BROOME	1990	
97 CILMERI	1998	
98 TULLOCH	2046	
99 LLANWRDA	2066	
100 ECCLES ROAD	2126	

101 BARROW HAVEN	2128	
102 LOCHAILORT	2186	
103 ST COLUMB ROAD	2188	
104 CAUSLAND	2198	
105 NORTH LLANRWST	2204	
106 LLANABER	2238	
107 MOSS SIDE	2328	
108 DUNSTON	2336	
109 LAPFORD	2354	
110 CHETNOLE	2398	
111 TAL-Y-CAFN	2400	
112 DALWHINNIE	2472	
113 LELANT	2494	
114 CORPACH	2532	
115 CHATHILL	2578	
116 CLAVERDON	2654	
117 THORNFORD	2708	
118 TONFANAU	2728	
119 NEWTON ST CYRES	2760	
120 ASCOTT-U-WYCHWOOD	2856	
121 LLANGENNECH	2908	
122 HOPTON HEATH	2990	
123 SALWICK	2994	
124 NEW LANE	3030	
125 RUSWARP	3032	
126 LOCH AWE	3034	
127 MONIFIETH	3122	
128 LLANGAMMARCH	3126	
=129 BESCAR LANE	3146	
=129 FFAIRFACH	3146	
131 OKEHAMPTON	3208	
132 HARLING ROAD	3222	
133 PENYCHAIN	3276	
134 SWINESHEAD	3294	
135 WENNINGTON	3378	
136 SALTMARSHE	3524	
137 GILFACH FARGOED	3690	
138 MANEA	3694	
139 KINGS'S NYMPTON	3748	
140 SWALE	3792	
141 BLEASBY	3798	
142 ROY BRIDGE	3856	
143 MAESTEG EWENNY RD	3930	
144 UPPER TYNDRUM	3940	
145 ACHNASHEEN	3972	
146 MENHENIOT	4064	
147 TYNDRUM LOWER	4082	
148 HAWARDEN BRIDGE	4088	
149 TY CROES	4142	
150 PEARTREE	4154	
151 ROLLESTON	4162
152 DOLWYDDELAN	4184
153 STYAL	4226
=154 DOVE HOLES	4382
=154 LLANDANWG	4382
156 CONNEL FERRY	4400
157 SLEIGHTS	4426
158 MANORS	4444
159 PENALLY	4506
160 ARDLUI	4566
161 GLAN CONWY	4572
162 MORAR	4626
163 DALMALLY	4632
164 GRIMSBY DOCKS	4662
165 INVERGOWRIE	4674
166 PONTARDDULAIS	4692
167 ST BUDEAUX FERRY RD	4754
=168 KNUCKLAS	4778
=168 PANTYFFYNNON	4778
=170 CASTLETON MOOR	4892
=170 PREES	4892
172 WIDDRINGTON	4962
173 LAMPHEY	4986
174 BLAYDON	5002
175 COMMONDALE	5026
176 GARVE	5028
177 SHIPTON	5050
178 GARELOCHHEAD	5256
179 LITTLE KIMBLE	5262
180 BURTON JOYCE	5302
181 NETHERFIELD	5382
182 CARRBRIDGE	5540
183 BODORGAN	5638
184 PONTEFRACT BAGHILL	5666
185 BANAVIE	5672
186 HELMSDALE	5778
187 BUCKNELL	5806
188 ASHLEY	5856
189 BRIDGE OF ORCHY	5932
190 PARTON	5948
191 LLANGADOG	6094
192 BRORA	6380
193 ALTHORPE	6404
194 FEARN	6606
195 WINCHELSEA	6640
196 SPEAN BRIDGE	6808
197 BUGLE	6810
198 GREAT AYTON	6826
199 PEVENSEY BAY	6838
200 THREE OAKS	6912

FIGURES ISSUED BY THE OFFICE OF RAIL REGULATION, ESTIMATES OF STATION USAGE 2013/2014 (DECEMBER 2014).

Britains Least Used Stations

INDEX

81 ABERERCH 3
203 ACHANALT 4
204 ACHNASHEEN 4
205 ACHNASHELLACH 4
64 ACKLINGTON 1
35 ALTHORPE 1
221 ALTNABRAEC 4
183 ARDLUI 4
82 ARDWICK 1
48 ARRAM 1
117 ASCOTT UNDER WYCHWOOD 2
93 ASHLEY 1
206 ATTADALE 4

176 BALMOSSIE 4
194 BANAVIE 4
71 BARLASTON 1
172 BARRHILL 4
30 BARROW HAVEN 1
178 BARRY LINKS 4
53 BATTERSBY 1
111 BEARLEY 2
199 BEASDALE 4
9 BERNEY ARMS 2
90 BESCAR LANE 1
59 BLAYDON 1
24 BLEASBY 2
85 BODORGAN 3
96 BRAYSTONES 1
173 BREICH 4
190 BRIDGE OF ORCHY 4
38 BRIGG 1
123 BROOME 3
31 BROOMFLEET 1
216 BRORA 4
8 BUCKENHAM 2
125 BUCKNELL 3
162 BUGLE 3
26 BURTON JOYCE 2
143 BYNEA 3

181 CARRBRIDGE 4
56 CASTLETON MOOR 1
159 CAUSELAND 3
153 CHAPELTON 3
65 CHATHILL 1
114 CHETNOLE 3
132 CILMERI 3
110 CLAVERDON 2
87 CLIFTON 1
115 COMBE 2
55 COMMONDALE 1
188 CONNEL FERRY 4
157 COOMBE JUNCTION HALT 3
195 CORPACH 4
211 CULRAIN 4
136 CYNGHORDY 3

185 DALMALLY 4
180 DALWHINNIE 4
46 DENT 1
84 DENTON 1
129 DOLAU 3
102 DOLGARROG 3
105 DOLWYDDELAN 3
92 DOVE HOLES 1
73 DOVEY JUNCTION 3
209 DUIRINISH 4
208 DUNCRAIG 4
215 DUNROBIN CASTLE 4
60 DUNSTON 1

32 EASTRINGTON 1
11 ECCLES ROAD 2
21 ELTON & ORSTON 2

187 FALLS OF CRUACHAN 4
210 FEARN 4
139 FFAIRFACH 3
116 FINSTOCK 2
220 FORSINARD 4

36 GAINSBOROUGH CENTRAL 1
182 GARELOCHHEAD 4
133 GARTH (POWYS) 3
201 GARVE 3
223 GEORGEMAS JUNCTION 4
144 GILFACH FARGOED 3
100 GLAN CONWY 3
179 GOLF STREET 4
52 GREAT AYTON 1
28 GRIMSBY DOCKS 1

12 HARLING ROAD 2
16 HAVENHOUSE 2
99 HAWARDEN BRIDGE 3
217 HELMSDALE 4
40 HENSALL 1
124 HOPTON HEATH 3
88 HOSCAR 1
18 HUBBERTS BRIDGE 2

107 INCE & ELTON 1
175 INVERGOWRIE 4
212 INVERSHIN 4

122 JOHNSTON 3

68 KEMPSTON HARDWICK 2
156 KEYHAM 3
54 KILDALE 1
218 KILDONAN 4
219 KINBRACE 4
151 KINGS NYMPTON 3
37 KIRTON LINDSEY 1
126 KNUCKLAS 3

236   Britains Least Used Stations

213 LAIRG 4
13 LAKENHEATH 2
121 LAMPHEY 3
150 LAPFORD 3
166 LELANT 3
109 LITTLE KIMBLE 2
75 LLANABER 3
128 LLANBISTER ROAD 3
77 LLANDANWG 3
79 LLANDECWYN 3
138 LLANGADOG 3
134 LLANGAMMARCH 3
142 LLANGENNECH 3
127 LLANGYNLLO 3
137 LLANWRDA 3
198 LOCHAILORT 4
186 LOCH AWE 4
196 LOCH EIL OUTWARD BOUND 4
197 LOCHEILSIDE 4
202 LOCHLUICHART 4
167 LONGCROSS 2
161 LUXULYAN 3

119 MAESTEG EWENNY ROAD 3
15 MANEA 2
61 MANORS 1
148 MENHENIOT 3
177 MONIFIETH 4
200 MORAR 4
94 MOSS SIDE 1

22 NETHERFIELD 2
97 NETHERTOWN 1
27 NEW CLEE 1
89 NEW LANE 1
149 NEWTON ST CYRES 3
103 NORTH LLANRWST 3
70 NORTON BRIDGE 1

155 OKEHAMPTON 3

140 PANTYFFYNNON 3
98 PARTON 1
67 PEARTREE 2
62 PEGSWOOD 1
120 PENALLY 3
76 PENSARN 3
131 PEN-Y-BONT 3
80 PENYCHAIN 3
168 PEVENSEY BAY 2
146 PILNING 3
69 POLESWORTH 2
141 PONTARDDULAIS 3
44 PONTEFRACT BAGHILL 1
104 PONT-Y-PANT 3
152 PORTSMOUTH ARMS 3
145 PREES 1

165 QUINTREL DOWNS 3

20 RAUCEBY 2
43 RAWCLIFFE 1
51 REDCAR BRITISH STEEL 1
83 REDDISH SOUTH 1
163 ROCHE 3
214 ROGART 4
23 ROLLESTON 2
106 ROMAN BRIDGE 3
192 ROY BRIDGE 4
58 RUSWARP 1

34 SALTMARSHE 1
95 SALWICK 1
154 SAMPFORD COURTENAY 3
160 SANDPLACE 3
222 SCOTSCALDER
14 SHIPPEA HILL 2
118 SHIPTON 2
57 SLEIGHTS 1
42 SNAITH 1
50 SOUTH BANK 1
193 SPEAN BRIDGE 4
174 SPRINGFIELD 4
10 SPOONER ROW 2
147 ST BUDEAUX FERRY ROAD 3
164 ST COLUMB ROAD 3
158 ST KEYNE WISHING WELL HALT 3
108 STANLOW & THORNTON 1
207 STROMEFERRY 4
91 STYAL 1
135 SUGAR LOAF 3
171 SWALE 2
19 SWINESHEAD 2

101 TAL-Y-CAFN 3
49 TEESSIDE AIRPORT 1
112 THORNFORD 3
29 THORNTON ABBEY 1
17 THORPE CULVERT 2
169 THREE OAKS 2
25 THURGARTON 2
74 TONFANAU 3
191 TULLOCH 4
86 TY CROES 3
78 TYGWYN 3
184 TYNDRUM LOWER 4

47 ULLESKELF 1
189 UPPER TYNDRUM 4

72 WEDGWOOD 1
45 WENNINGTON 1
39 WHITLEY BRIDGE 1
63 WIDDRINGTON 1
170 WINCHELSEA 2
33 WRESSLE 1

113 YETMINSTER 3

Britains Least Used Stations